FABLES OF AGGRESSION

FABLES OF AGGRESSION

Wyndham Lewis, the Modernist as Fascist

Fredric Jameson

UNIVERSITY OF CALIFORNIA PRESS
Berkeley / Los Angeles / London

Title page illustration: Wyndham Lewis, *The Cept*, 1921.
Copyright Mrs. G. A. Wyndham Lewis. Used by permission.

Initials at chapter openings adapted from the *Vorticist Alphabet*,
designed by Edward Wadsworth in 1919.

A draft of the first chapters appeared in *Hudson Review*,
Volume xxvi, Number 2 (Summer, 1973).

University of California Press
Berkeley and Los Angeles, California

University of California Press, Ltd.
London, England

ISBN 0-520-03792-8
Library of Congress Catalog Card Number: 78-64462
Printed in the United States of America

1 2 3 4 5 6 7 8 9

For George Herring

Contents /

References /

Page references to the following editions of Lewis' works will be given in the text, under these abbreviations:

AG   *The Apes of God.* London: Penguin Books, 1965.

CM   *The Childermass,* Volume I of *The Human Age.* London: Calder, 1965.

MF   *Malign Fiesta,* Volume III of *The Human Age.* London: Calder and Boyars, 1966.

MG   *Monstre gai,* Volume II of *The Human Age.* London: Calder, 1965.

RL   *The Revenge for Love.* Chicago: Henry Regnery, 1952.

SC   *Self Condemned.* Chicago: Henry Regnery, 1965.

SH   *The Soldier of Humour and Selected Writings.* New York: New American Library, 1966.

T   *Tarr* (second version). London: Calder and Boyars, 1968.

TWM   *Time and Western Man.* Boston: Beacon, 1957.

Prologue /
ON NOT READING
WYNDHAM LEWIS

DEOLOGY, PSYCHOANALYSIS, NARRATIVE analysis: these are the coordinates within which the following study seeks to construct an interpretive model of one of the most striking, ambiguous and little known bodies of fiction produced in English in recent times, a corpus which explicitly demands such interpretative frameworks by its brutal foregrounding of politics and sex and its ostentatious practice of style.

Wyndham Lewis is surely the least read and most unfamiliar of all the great modernists of his generation, a generation that included the names of Pound and Eliot, Joyce, Lawrence and Yeats; nor can it be said that his painting has been assimilated any more successfully into the visual canon.[1] Lewis was a presence for his contem-

1. But the reader can now consult *Wyndham Lewis: Paintings and Drawings*, ed. Walter Michel (Berkeley and Los Angeles: University of California Press, 1971).

1

poraries, but we have forgotten their admiration for him. At best, in Britain today, he retains a kind of national celebrity and is read as a more scandalous and explosive Waugh; while internationally his name remains a dead letter, despite the diligent efforts of Hugh Kenner and others to make a place for him in some Pound-centered modern pantheon.[2]

Yet it has been my experience that new readers can be electrified by exposure to *Tarr*, a book in which, as in few others, the sentence is reinvented with all the force of origins, as sculptural gesture and fiat in the void. Such reinvention, however, demands new reading habits, for which we are less and less prepared. Anglo-American modernism has indeed traditionally been dominated by an impressionistic aesthetic, rather than that—externalizing and mechanical—of Lewis' expressionism. The most influential formal impulses of canonical modernism have been strategies of inwardness, which set out to reappropriate an alienated universe by transforming it into personal styles and private languages: such wills to style have seemed in retrospect to reconfirm the very privatization and fragmentation of social life against which they meant to protest.

So it is that the initial, passionately subversive force of the modernist symbolic act is ever fainter and more distant for the contemporary reader, within the *société de consom-*

2. The first books on Lewis are still the best introductions: H. G. Porteus, *Wyndham Lewis: A Discursive Exposition* (London: Desmond Harmsworth, 1932); and Hugh Kenner, *Wyndham Lewis* (Norfolk, Ct.: New Directions, 1954), which should be supplemented by his more recent essays on *The Human Age* ("The Devil and Wyndham Lewis," in *Gnomon* [New York: McDowell, Obolensky, 1958]) and on Lewis's painting, his introduction ("The Visual World of Wyndham Lewis") in Michel, *Paintings and Drawings*. A brief listing of the meager critical literature is to be found in R. T. Chapman, *Wyndham Lewis: Fiction and Satires* (London: Vision Press, 1973). D. G. Bridson, *The Filibusterer* (London: Cassell, 1972), provides a useful review of Lewis' political positions in their historical contexts. My debt to Robert C. Elliott, *The Power of Satire* (Princeton: Princeton University Press, 1960), and in particular to the Lewis chapter, will become evident later on. The liveliest book on Lewis, however, remains his own autobiography, *Rude Assignment* (London: Hutchinson, 1950).

mation with its various postmodernisms; and this not least because the modernist canon has itself become classical, institutionalized within the university, its stylistic innovations meanwhile fully integrated into the commodity system with its ever increasing momentum of style—and fashion—change. If it is idle to deplore, as Trilling does in *Beyond Culture,* the loss or repression of that original antisocial resonance of the great modernisms,[3] it is on the other hand a matter of some historical gratification to come upon a modernism which is still extant and breathing, an archaic survival, like the antediluvian creatures of Conan Doyle's *Lost World* hidden away within a forgotten fold of the earth's surface. The neglect of Lewis is thus a happy accident for us, who can then, as from out of a time capsule, once more sense that freshness and virulence of modernizing stylization less and less accessible in the faded texts of his contemporaries.

There were of course excellent and objective reasons for Lewis' neglect: reasonable motives, which it would be naive to ignore, for the resistance of sophisticated modern readers to that particular brand of modernism he had in store for them. A consistent perversity made of him at one and the same time the exemplary practitioner of one of the most powerful of all modernistic styles and an aggressive ideological critic and adversary of modernism itself in all its forms. Indeed, *Time and Western Man* (1927) diagnostically attributes the aberrant impulse of all the great contemporary artistic and philosophical modernisms to what he called the "Time Cult," to the fetishization of temporality and the celebration of Bergsonian flux. However illuminating this diagnosis may have been, it had the unfortunate effect of forcing his readership to choose between

3. Complaining of what he calls "the socialization of the anti-social, the acculturation of the anti-cultural, or the legitimization of the subversive," Trilling adds: "when the term-essays come in, it is plain to me that almost none of the students have been taken aback by what they have read: they have almost wholly contained the attack. . . ." *Beyond Culture* (New York: Viking, 1965), p. 26.

himself and virtually everything else (Joyce, Pound, Proust, Stein, Picasso, Stravinsky, Bergson, Whitehead, etc.) in the modern canon.

Meanwhile, at the very moment in which the modernisms of the mainstream discovered their anti-Victorian vocation and developed a battery of onslaughts on moral taboos and repressive hypocrisies, an analogous gesture finds Lewis affirming the oppressiveness of the sexual instinct and unseasonably expressing a kind of archaic horror at sexual dependency. The polemic hostility to feminism, the uglier misogynist fantasies embodied in his narratives, the obsessive phobia against homosexuals, the most extreme restatements of grotesque traditional sexist myths and attitudes—such features, released by Lewis' peculiar sexual politics and abundantly documented in the following pages, are not likely to endear him to the contemporary reader.

This *esprit de contradiction* of Lewis' polemic and aesthetic production alike is but another face of that aggressivity which was a lifelong constant of both the form and the content of his works, and of his own characterological style. To the aggressive impulses Lewis found within himself we are of course indebted for the astonishing pathology of figures like Kreisler (in *Tarr*). But there is no point denying the oppressiveness with which such impulses gradually become dominant, are generalized and projected outwards as a global hostility, not merely to his own characters, but also to the quasi-totality of his contemporaries as well, not excluding his own readership. The latter may therefore be forgiven occasional reactions like that of Hemingway to the real-life Lewis.[4] On the stylistic level, such intransigence drives the more experimental texts to

4. "I do not think I had ever seen a nastier-looking man . . . . Under the black hat, when I had first seen them, the eyes had been those of an unsuccessful rapist" (*A Moveable Feast* [New York: Scribners, 1964], p. 109). This is perhaps the place to say that it strikes me as disingenuous to read Lewis' work, as John Holloway does, in *The Charted Mirror* (London: Routledge & Kegan Paul, 1960), as the *critique* of violence rather than as its expression.

extremes which make some of them virtually unreadable for any sustained period of time (this is at least my own current feeling about *The Apes of God* [1930]).

Ideologically, Lewis' brief flirtation with Nazism—celebrated in the notorious *Hitler* (1931)[5]—stands as a symptom somewhere in between his deep misogyny and his violent anti-Communism. The episode itself may have been no more (but no less) serious than the comparable enthusiasms of Pound, Yeats, Shaw and others; yet it entitles us to raise the issue of our title—the affinities between protofascism and Western modernism—on the occasion of a work that continues to enlighten us about this subject even after Lewis' repentant conversion to more socially acceptable forms of anti-Communism, most notably with his fellow-travelling adherence to Roman Catholicism during World War II. The stance of the postwar polemics—see, for instance, *The Writer and The Absolute* (1952), a blistering attack on Sartrean *engagement* and the concept of a political vocation for literature—only reconfirmed his sterile and chronic oppositionalism, his cranky and passionate mission to repudiate whatever in "modern civilization" seemed to be currently fashionable. The more sombre and dramatic turns in Lewis' personal destiny—his forced and impecunious exile in Canada during World War II, the blindness visited on the great painter during his final years—do not necessarily redeem the querulous posture of the nay-sayer or make it any more immediately attractive to the unfamiliar reader.

In spite of all this—yet in some deeper sense, surely, because of it—Lewis' intellectual, formal, and ideological trajectory was marked and monumentalized by a series of remarkable novels, each one utterly unlike the next, and all of them without analogy among the production of his contemporaries. We have already mentioned his "artist's novel," *Tarr* (written in 1914, and published in two ver-

5. London: Chatto & Windus, 1931. See Appendix for an account of this work.

sions, in 1918 and 1928). The mid-thirties Graham-Greene-type thriller, *The Revenge for Love* (1937), invests Bolshevik conspiracies with a characteristic and unmistakably personal resonance. The autobiographical *Self Condemned* (1954), bleakest of all Lewis' works, records the dark night of the soul in the icy dreariness of exile in wartime Canada. Finally, spanning thirty years, the immense unfinished *Human Age* (whose first volume, *The Childermass* [1928] constitutes a veritable summa of Lewis' narrative modernism) unexpectedly confronts us with the supreme realization of what has to be called theological science fiction.

Such texts, which reveal Lewis to have been among the most richly inventive of modern British writers, merit unapologetic rediscovery and can sustain enthusiastic reading as well as the closest critical scrutiny. Yet the juxtaposition of their formal innovation with the ideological and libidinal content identified above raises issues of a more theoretical nature and confronts us with interpretive and methodological problems which we must now address.

The present study takes as its object what I have elsewhere called the "political unconscious" in Lewis' works, thus necessarily obliging us to make connections between the findings of narrative analysis, psychoanalysis, and traditional as well as modern approaches to ideology. The methodological eclecticism with which such a project can be reproached is unavoidable, since the discontinuities projected by these various disciplines or methods themselves correspond to objective discontinuities in their object (and beyond that, to the very fragmentation and compartmentalization of social reality in modern times). It is therefore less important to justify a disparate range of theoretical references than it is to take some initial inventory of the objective gaps and disjunctions within the texts themselves.

First and foremost among such discontinuities is surely that formal incommensurability which confronts the reader of any modern text, but which is usefully exasperated by

those under study here, and which we can convey in terms
of the unsatisfactory alternative between stylistics and narrative analysis, or in other words, between the micro- and
the macro-level of cultural artifacts. Every serious practic-
ing critic knows a secret which is less often publicly discussed, namely, that there exists no ready-made corridor
between the sealed chamber of stylistic investigation and
that equally unventilated space in which the object of
study is reconstituted as narrative structure. In practice,
whatever the solution adopted, there is always an uncomfortable shifting of gears in the movement from one of
these perspectives to the other: nor does the assertion of
this or that "homology" between style and narrative do
much more than to pronounce resolved in advance the dilemma for which it was supposed to provide a working
answer.

To grasp this discontinuity as an objective reality in
our culture, rather than as a methodological inconsistency
which might be solved by tinkering with the methods in
question and readjusting them to each other, requires us
radically to historicize the gap between style and narrative,
which then may be seen as an event in the history of form.
The name of Flaubert is a useful marker for this development, in which the two "levels" of the narrative text begin
to drift apart and acquire their own relative autonomy; in
which the rhetorical and instrumental subordination of
narrative language to narrative representation can no
longer be taken for granted. The plotless art novel and the
styleless bestseller can then be seen as the end products of
this tendency, which corresponds to the antithesis between
what, following Deleuze and Guattari,[6] we will call the
molecular and the *molar* impulses in modern form-

6. Gilles Deleuze and Felix Guattari, *Anti-Oedipus: Capitalism and Schizophrenia*, translated by Robert Hurley, Mark Seem and Helen R. Lane (New
York: Viking, 1977), pp. 273–296 (and also pp. 1–50). In what follows, this
provocative and layered book will essentially be used as an *aesthetic*, that is, as
the description of and apologia for a new type of discourse: the discontinuous,
"schizophrenic" text.

production no less than in contemporary social life itself. In this use, the molecular level designates the here-and-now of immediate perception or of local desire, the production-time of the individual sentence, the electrifying shock of the individual word or the individual brushstroke, of the regional throb of pain or of pleasure, the sudden obsessive, cathected, fascination or the equally immediate repulsion of Freudian decathexis. To this microscopic, fragmentary life of the psyche in the immediate a counterforce is opposed in the molar (from *moles,* the mass of molecules organized into larger organic unities), which designates all those large, abstract, mediate, and perhaps even empty and imaginary forms by which we seek to recontain the molecular: the mirage of the continuity of personal identity, the organizing unity of the psyche or the personality, the concept of society itself, and, not least, the notion of the organic unity of the work of art. This distinction allows us to respect the specificity of the narrative level, while grasping its function to recontain the molecular proliferation of sentences on the stylistic level.

We will therefore read Lewis' sentence-production as a symbolic act in its own right, an explosive and window-breaking *praxis* on the level of the words themselves. The narratives on that view become what the Russian Formalists would have called the "motivation of the device," that is, the formal pretext which enables such stylistic production and lends it justification after the fact. Yet considered on its own terms, Lewis' molar forms, the macrologic of his narratives, prove to have a very different dynamic from the momentum of the sentences themselves: what was in the latter sheer production and energy now veers about into the negative element, into an intolerable closure, an atmosphere of violence and destruction which the narratives articulate into a self-perpetuating sequence of rape, physical assault, aggressivity, guilt and immolation.

At this point, the molar level, the narrative frame,

must be the object of a different kind of investigation, one which requires as its precondition some acknowledgement of the objective status of this new level.

To invoke psychoanalysis and ideology at this stage is not to suggest that we have left behind the discontinuities and methodological double standards that plague stylistics. Here too, on the contrary, the antithesis between the apparently distinct realms of the sexual and the political, between childhood and society, archaic fantasy and ideological commitment, infantile wish-fulfillment and adult "value," reflects an objective dissociation in contemporary experience. At the same time it projects and reinforces a whole psychologizing and subjectivizing ideology deeply engrained in American society: wherever a depth-psychological "explanation" of political commitment is invoked, indeed, we may be sure that the end product of the operation will be a reduction of the political to the psychological, a transformation of the former into so many "projections" to which the clinical response can only be the "adaptation" of the individual to some more "realistic" assessment of an outer world, now locked like a thing-in-itself outside personal experience.

To such a dilemma, the "repudiation" of the findings of psychoanalysis seems an inadequate, if not an impossible, solution.[7] I would suggest that the situation is fundamentally modified if we insist on isolating from that properly psychoanalytic material (in which, particularly in Freud's own work, it plays so decisive a part) an autonomous narrative moment or "instance" with a specificity and a dynamism of its own. To isolate an independent narrative function in psychic life is then to win some distance from the ruses by which the unconscious can be seen to make use of it. This is the signal advantage of the model which has been our working solution in the following

---

7. This is, however, exactly what Deleuze and Guattari propose, in those parts of their book which attack the concept of the Oedipus complex.

study, and which, following J.-F. Lyotard, we will call the "libidinal apparatus."[8]

The semi-autonomy or objectivity of this model makes for practical consequences which are quite distinct from those of analogous formulations in earlier theory, which range from Charles Mauron's notion of the "personal myth" developed in a writer's *oeuvre* to Frye's more Jungian concept of the narrative archetype.[9] The first inevitably drives narrative production back into the history of the individual psyche; the second, by positioning the social and collective dimension of narrative at the beginning of history, short-circuits the complicated process whereby an empty narrative schema becomes invested with concrete social and ideological content. The theory of the libidinal apparatus marks an advance over psychologizing approaches in the way in which it endows a private fantasy-structure with a quasi-material inertness, with all the resistance of an object which can lead a life of its own and has its own inner logic and specific dynamics. Such a view then allows us to understand its various uses and investments as a process of appropriation and reappropriation, as a structure which, produced by the accidents of a certain history, can be alienated and pressed into the service of a quite different one, reinvested with new and unexpected content, and adapted to unsuspected ideological functions which return upon the older psychic material to re- or overdetermine it in its turn as a kind of retroactive effect (Freud's *Nachträglichkeit*). On such a view, then, the libid-

8. See Jean-François Lyotard, *Des dispositifs pulsionnels* (Paris: 10/18, 1973) and *Économie libidinale* (Paris: Editions de Minuit, 1974). The useful French term "dispositif" is unfortunately untranslatable. For Lyotard the "dispositif" is what captures and immobilizes desire, rather than as in my use, what allows it investment and articulation. Lyotard's emphasis is on the ways in which "desire" breaks through such "dispositifs," rather than on the social and historical conditions of possibility of the libidinal apparatus.

9. Charles Mauron, *Des métaphores obsédantes au mythe personnel* (Paris: Corti, 1962); and Northrop Frye, *The Anatomy of Criticism* (Princeton: Princeton University Press, 1957).

inal apparatus becomes an independent structure of which one can write a history: and this history—the story of the logical permutations of a given fantasy-structure, as well as of its approaches to its own closure and internal limits—is a very different one from that projected by the conventional literary psychoanalysis or psycho-biography, which take as their object of study something to which we no longer have access, and which is therefore here bracketed from the outset, namely the private psyche of the biographical individual, Wyndham Lewis himself.[10]

The concept of the libidinal apparatus will indeed allow us to reverse the traditional priorities of psychoanalytic and psychologizing interpretation. In particular, it will lead us to the conclusion that the objective preconditions of the narrative structures that inform Lewis' imagination, far from being familial or archaic, are rather to be sought in a very different space, namely in the objective configurations of the political history of pre-1914 Europe. We will see that it is the diplomatic system of the pre-War nation-states which provides a narrative apparatus, an objectified fantasy-structure, only thereafter reinvested and over-determined by the libidinal and the instinctual. This seemingly untestable hypothesis is then dramatically and as it were experimentally "verified" by History itself, which, with the Great War, dislocates the older diplomatic system and effectively prepares a wholly new force field, in which, not the older nation-states, but rather the great new emergent and transnational forces of Communism and Fascism, become the "subjects of history." Or such a momentous upheaval, the narrative system of *Tarr* is a striking casualty; and the formal "break" whereby on its ruins there emerges, in Lewis' post-War work, a whole new libidinal apparatus, a new psychic "energy" model as well as a whole new ideological dynamic, will indeed be the central story the present book has to tell.

10. Lewis' work, however, cries out for a psychobiography of the quality of those of Sartre or Erikson.

Yet it should not be thought that traditional ideological analysis is any less problematic than psychoanalysis in its repression or "denial" of the narrative instance. If you believe that ideology is essentially a matter of conceptual positions, opinions, attitudes and values, then ideological analysis reduces itself to a typologizing and classificatory affair, a labelling operation, in which we are called on to "decide" whether it is fair to assign Lewis' work to the category marked "fascist," or whether it would not be more adequate to identify him simply as an "anti-liberal" or "classical conservative."

The conception of ideology which informs the present study is quite different from this, and may be seen as a practical exploration of Althusser's seminal definition of the ideological as "a 'representation' of the Imaginary relationship of individuals to their real conditions of existence."[11] Two features of this definition need to be retained: first, that ideology must always be necessarily narrative in its structure, inasmuch as it not only involves a mapping of the real, but also the essentially narrative or fantasy attempt of the subject to invent a place for himself/herself in a collective and historical process which excludes him or her and which is itself basically nonrepresentable and nonnarrative. This is the sense of Althusser's otherwise scandalous description of History as a "process without a subject or a *telos*,"[12] and leads us to the second important implication of the definition in question. For the "Real" on this view is conceived, neither as an unknowable thing-in-itself, nor as a string of events or set of facts you can know directly in the form of some "true" or "adequate" representation for consciousness. It is rather an asymptotic phenomenon, an outer limit, which the subject ap-

11. Louis Althusser, *Lenin and Philosophy*, translated by Ben Brewster, (London: New Left Books, 1971), p. 162.
12. Louis Althusser, "Reply to John Lewis," in *Essays in Self-Criticism* (London: New Left Books), translated by Grahame Lock, p. 99.

proaches in the anxiety of the moment of truth—moments of personal crisis and of the agonizing political polarization of revolutionary situations; and from such an approach to the Real the subject then tends to retreat again, at best in possession of abstract or purely intellectual schemata when not of personally charged narrative representations. The narrative apparatus which informs ideological representations is thus not mere "false consciousness," but an authentic way of grappling with a Real that must always transcend it, a Real into which the subject seeks to insert itself through praxis, all the while painfully learning the lesson of its own ideological closure and of history's resistance to the fantasy-structures in which it is itself locked.

This is the moment to return to our title, and to the twin issues of modernism and fascism which, not without a certain provocation, it raises. The theory of modernism presupposed here may briefly be characterized as a critique and synthesis all at once of the two great rival theories of modernism current today.[13] On one side, we inevitably confront Lukács' apologia for nineteenth-century realism, in which modernism is denounced as the symptom and reflex of the reification of late capitalist social relations. On the other, equally predictably, we find ranged in order the various ideologists of the modern itself, all the way from the great Anglo-American and Russian modernists to Adorno and the Tel Quel group: for them, the formal innovations of modernism are to be understood as essentially revolutionary acts, and in particular as the repudiation of the values of a business society and of its characteristic representational categories (nature, the organic work of art, mimesis, and so forth).

---

13. See, for a more general outline of these positions, my "Reflections in Conclusion," to the collection of materials on the so-called Brecht-Lukács debate, *Aesthetics and Politics* (London: New Left Books, 1977), pp. 196–213.

If, however, reification is grasped as a concrete historical situation and a dilemma, then these two positions cease to be as inconsistent as they first appeared. On this view, reification may be seen as a fragmentation of the psyche and of its world that opens up the semi-autonomous and henceforth compartmentalized spaces of lived time over against clock time, bodily or perceptual experience over against rational and instrumental consciousness, a realm of "originary" or creative language over against the daily practice of a degraded practical speech, the space of the sexual and the archaic over against the reality- and performance-principles of "le sérieux" and of adult life, and of the growing independence of the various senses from one another—in particular the separation of the eye from the ear.

Ultimately of course, this fragmentation generates a psychic division of labor which reorders all the others into a fundamental opposition between the subject and the object, between the private or the psychological and a henceforth inert scientifically and technologically manipulable external "reality." But if this is the case, then it becomes clear that modernism not only reflects and reinforces such fragmentation and commodification of the psyche as its basic precondition, but that the various modernisms all seek to overcome that reification as well, by the exploration of a new Utopian and libidinal experience of the various sealed realms or psychic compartments to which they are condemned, but which they also reinvent. Lewis' "modernism"—but also, as we shall see, his "fascism"— is to be understood as just such a protest against the reified experience of an alienated social life, in which, against its own will, it remains formally and ideologically locked.

As for fascism, it is evident that Lewis was in no sense an official fascist ideologue, of the type of French collaborators like Drieu la Rochelle or Brasillach, or the Nazi and Italian intellectuals. At best, his brief flirtation with

Nazism offers an instructive glimpse into the complex ideological appeal of what can best be called protofascism, which we must now replace in its historical context. Protofascism may be characterized as a shifting strategy of class alliances whereby an initially strong populist and anticapitalist impulse is gradually readapted to the ideological habits of a petty bourgeoisie, which can itself be displaced when, with the consolidation of the fascist state, effective power passes back into the hands of big business.[14]

The constitutive elements of protofascism as a cultural and ideological phenomenon are four-fold: (1) Throughout its evolution, it remains a reaction to and a defense against the continuing ideological threat and presence of a (defeated) Marxism, which thus occupies that taboo position around which the various fascist ideologies must organize themselves. (2) Its elaboration as an ideology is, however, determined less by the practical dangers of Marxism or Communism than by the disintegration and functional discrediting—even after the failure of revolution on the Left—of the various hegemonic and legitimizing ideologies of the middle class state (liberalism, conservatism, Catholicism, social democracy, etc.). If therefore as a reaction-formation it defines itself against Marxism as the fundamental enemy, protofascism grasps itself consciously as the implacable critique of the various middle class ideologies and of the parliamentary system in which they find representation. (3) The structural inconsistency of these first two features opens up an ambiguous space in which a critique of capitalism can be displaced and inflected in the direction of the characteristic features of classical petty-bourgeois ideology (see below). (4) Finally, these various free-floating attitudes must be given practical embodiment in a mass ideological party which can stand as a figure for

14. Nicos Poulantzas, *Fascism and Dictatorship* (London: New Left Books, 1974), esp. pp. 66–67, and 252–256. For a critical review of theories of fascism, see Martin Kitchen, *Fascism* (London: Macmillan, 1976).

the new collectivity at the same time that it serves as the vehicle for the seizure of state power. In this, protofascism distinguishes itself from Caesarism—the *coup d'état* of the isolated charismatic hero—and once more affirms its reactive stance towards Marxism, insofar as the original model of the party apparatus is a Leninist and Bolshevik innovation.

We will see that all of these features find a specifically narrative or structural place in Lewis' narrative system or "libidinal apparatus." For the moment, it seems useful to identify their presence in his work in a more static and schematic way. We will, for example, argue that Lewis' "populist" component is expressed through his stylistic practice, itself mediated by the excitement of the machine and of a mechanical production which effectively distances his "modernism" from other artisanal or hierophantic modernist aesthetics.

His fascination with the mass ideological party—particularly in *The Childermass*—has a significant structural influence on the emergence of the later transindividual libidinal apparatus, in which characters are little more than the bearers, or vehicles, of great collective and ideological forces. In particular, the emphasis on the collective generates a unique new narrative form—what we have called theological science fiction—which "includes history" more adequately than the Poundian epic or the Joycean universal mythography.

Meanwhile, the "petty-bourgeois" stance in Lewis' work can best be detected in the obsessive formal problem of the social and narrative place to be assigned to the essentially placeless observer/satirist. All the classical descriptions of petty-bourgeois ideology have stressed the way in which the structural instability of this "class" (neither proletariat nor classical bourgeoisie, let alone big business; living in the permanent anxiety of proletarianization) inscribes itself in its thought in the form of what

Barthes has called its "neither-nor-ism,"[15] in its mirage of social harmony (archetypally dramatized by the class handshake at the end of Lang's *Metropolis*), and in the valorization of those purely intellectual skills—science, education, bureaucratic service—which might lend it a non-class-based legitimation. The ideological defense of culture, in particular, explains the potential usefulness of the petty-bourgeois stance as a working ideology for intellectuals at the same time that it accounts for the attractiveness of the state itself for the petty bourgeoisie, which it projects, in its own image, as an arbiter above the social classes.

We will suggest that Lewis lived a grinding contradiction between his aggressive critical, polemic and satiric impulses and his unwillingness to identify himself with any determinate class position or ideological commitment: at this point it is enough to mention his ultimate fall-back position, which asserts the ultimate critical standard and Archimedean point of the pure eye and attempts to justify his immense and wide-ranging cultural critiques in terms

15. Roland Barthes, *Mythologies*, translated by Annette Lavers (New York. Hill & Wang, 1972), p. 153. The reader should be reminded that Marx's own model of ideology is not one of 'false consciousness' or of class origins, but rather stresses the structural limits or ideological closure imposed on thought by its class positioning within the social totality. In his classical account of petty-bourgeois ideology (drawn on by all later versions like this one of Barthes), Marx observes: "Just as little must one imagine that the democratic representatives [to the Legislative Assembly of 1849] are indeed all shopkeepers or enthusiastic champions of shopkeepers. According to their education and their individual position they may be as far apart as heaven from earth. What makes them representatives of the petty bourgeoisie is the fact that in their minds they do not get beyond the limits which the latter do not get beyond in life, that they are consequently driven, theoretically, to the same problems and solutions to which material interest and social position drive the latter politically. This is, in general, the relationship between the *political* and *literary representatives* of a class and the class they represent" (*The Eighteenth Brumaire of Louis Bonaparte* [New York: International, 1963], pp. 50–51). The most extended "application" or practical "demonstration" of this theory of ideological closure remains Lukács' analysis of German Idealist philosophy ("The Antinomies of Bourgeois Thought," in *History and Class Consciousness*, translated by Rodney Livingstone, [Cambridge, Mass.: MIT Press, 1971], pp. 110–149).

of the defense of the rights of the visual and the painter's practice. This untenable squaring of the circle allows him to repress the structural center of his work, which lies not in the position of the observing subject, but rather in his implacable lifelong opposition to Marxism itself.

Finally, his violent critique and repudiation of all of the hegemonic ideologies of the parliamentary bourgeois state may be taken as a figure for the crisis and fragmentation of the subject itself. The articulation of this crisis of the subject in the objective form of a protofascist denunciation of parliamentary corruption, however, provides Lewis with an active and aggressive system of figuration which is quite distinct from its more symptomatic and subjectivizing expression (solipsism, the monad, schizophrenic dissolution) in conventional modernism. In this framework, meanwhile, the damaged subject can itself know objective figuration of a type quite different from the pathos of the conventional antihero, in Lewis' identification with post-Versailles Germany as underdog and victim.

This checklist is not yet to be understood as an ideological analysis of Lewis, but rather merely as the social, historical and conceptual framework within which such analysis—a narrative and structural examination rather than a classificatory operation—can eventually be undertaken. Yet we cannot begin without some final word on the literary and cultural value of Lewis' work and on the reasons that may remain for reading it after so apparently thoroughgoing an ideological arraignment as has just been made. This question is all the more urgent in view of the often affirmed incapacity of historicist—and most particularly Marxist—criticism to develop a theory of aesthetic value. To such a theory, then, the following three concluding observations may be offered as a contribution.

It is first of all a commonplace of Marxist historiography that the initial critiques of the nascent world of market capitalism emerge on the Right: in this sense, Edmund Burke's seminal assault on Jacobinism can be read, less as a denunciation of social revolution, than as an anticipatory critique of emergent bourgeois social life; while the later Romantic and conservative critiques of nineteenth century culture recapitulate in advance much of the Marxian diagnosis of alienation, commodification, and reification, albeit from a nostalgic and regressive standpoint. It is therefore no surprise to find that Lewis' polemics—and the protofascist critiques of capitalism to which they are related—have much the same ambiguous critical and negative force. The attacks on subjectivism, on establishment modernism, on the "Time Cult" and the "Youth Cult," on the illusions of the stable subject or ego, on the ideological dishonesty of hegemonic liberalism, are indeed more powerful and damaging than anything formulated by the Marxism of that period. In this sense, the continuing vitality of Lewis' work confirms the proposition of the Frankfurt School that the aesthetic value of works of art is directly proportional to their systematic formal repudiation of the fallen world of empirical being, of reified appearance and of the status quo.

Yet it is not only the "general ideology" of the period —to use Terry Eagleton's convenient distinction[16]—which is systematically unmasked and undermined in the work of Wyndham Lewis: the latter also very specifically and through its idiosyncratic practice of stylistic and formal production calls into question a dominant "aesthetic ideology" as well. We will have frequent occasion to observe the way in which that repudiation of the hegemonic naturalist and representational conventions which he shares with other modernisms is in Lewis reduplicated by a prophetic assault on the very conventions of the emergent modernisms themselves, which will become hegemonic in their turn only after World War II. This is the place to note some striking similarities between Lewis' undertak-

16. Terry Eagleton, *Criticism and Ideology* (London: New Left Books, 1976), pp. 54–60.

ing and the contemporary poststructuralist aesthetic, which signals the dissolution of the modernist paradigm—with its valorization of myth and symbol, temporality, organic form and the concrete universal, the identity of the subject and the continuity of linguistic expression—and foretells the emergence of some new, properly postmodernist or schizophrenic conception of the cultural artifact—now strategically reformulated as "text" or "écriture," and stressing discontinuity, allegory, the mechanical, the gap between signifier and signified, the lapse in meaning, the syncope in the experience of the subject. Lewis cannot be fully assimilated to the contemporary textual aesthetic without anachronism: we will indeed want to insist on the ways in which these tendencies are over and over again strategically recontained in his work. Yet any historicizing approach must reckon our own situation, our own present as observers, judges and actors, back into our evaluation of the past; and the approach of a postindividualistic age argues powerfully for the discovery of Lewis' kinship with us.

Still, neither of these propositions addresses the most urgent and visceral issue for any reader, namely, why he or she should be expected to find aesthetic pleasure and satisfaction in a work whose impulses are often so ugly or ideologically offensive. This is no mere question of personal taste but rather a fundamental aesthetic problem; a problem intensified by the presence, alongside the expression of this or that overt political opinion, alongside the lifelong affirmation of the intellectual inequality of human beings and the even more disturbing fascination with racial categories, of that obsessive sexism and misogyny which can go unnoticed by no reader of Lewis' work, or of the following pages. I wonder if I will be understood when I suggest that Lewis' expression of this particular *idée fixe* is so extreme as to be virtually beyond sexism. Misogyny in Lewis no longer exists at the level of mere personal opinion, as is the case, for example, with the various attitudes and "ideas" of a Balzac or a Faulkner, whose narratives so often function as vehicles for some irrepressible authorial intervention. Indeed, the stable subject or ego which could alone "entertain" such opinions has in Lewis been dissolved, so that they come before us in a virtually free-floating state, as unbound impulses released from the rationalizing censorship of a respectable consciousness intent on keeping up appearances.

In Lewis, therefore, such impulses are freed to acquire their own figuration; his artistic integrity is to be conceived, not as something distinct from his regrettable ideological lapses (as when we admire his art, *in spite of* his opinions), but rather in the very intransigence with which he makes himself the impersonal registering apparatus for forces which he means to record, beyond any whitewashing and liberal revisionism, in all their primal ugliness. In this sense Lewis is an exemplary manifestation of Althusser's account of the way in which art uses and transcends its ideological raw materials:

> What art makes us *see*, and therefore gives us in the form of *'seeing'*, *'perceiving'* and *'feeling'* (which is not the form of *knowing*) is the *ideology* from which it is born, in which it bathes, from which it detaches itself as art, and to which it alludes. . . . Balzac and Solzhenitsyn give us a 'view' of the ideology to which their work alludes and with which it is constantly fed, a view which presupposes a *retreat*, an *internal distantiation*, from the very ideology from which their novels emerged. They make us 'perceive' (but not know) in some sense *from the inside*, the very ideology in which they are held.[17]

The scandalous content of Lewis' work, however, offers a more acid test of this proposition than anything in Balzac's dead royalism or Solzhenitsyn's orthodox mysticism.

Yet in this form, Althusser's position remains a mere

---

17. Louis Althusser, "A Letter on Art," in *Lenin and Philosophy*, pp. 222–223.

hypothesis; and it is in the work of his collaborator, Pierre Macherey, that we can observe a more developed and suggestive model of the process by which the work of art can be said to "produce" the ideological as an object for our aesthetic contemplation and our political judgement. Macherey demonstrates that the very process whereby the ideological achieves objective figuration—in the form of language, narrative, character systems and the like—may be grasped as an intrinsically negative and critical "distantiation" of its ideological starting point, rather than its simple replication. The presupposition is that ideology as we know it must necessarily always be contradictory, and thereby ultimately incapable of coherent figural expression. To use his central illustration, Jules Verne's "conception" of the future is in reality to be grasped as a way of *not* conceptualizing the future: less the expression of the "idea" of progress than an imaginary and contradictory attempt to resolve the antinomies which the bourgeoisie of the Third Republic shrouded beneath the name of this ostensible concept. Yet not Verne's "thought," but his narrative structure betrays this effort, of which Macherey shows that its movement towards an impossible future is always recontained by the repetitive return to an archaic past, to the dead father, and the cyclical time of trauma and regression.[18]

We will therefore want to complete Althusser's explanation of aesthetic value by a methodological proposition: namely, that great art distances ideology by the way in which, endowing the latter with figuration and with narrative articulation, the text frees its ideological content to

18. See Pierre Macherey, *Pour une théorie de la production littéraire* (Paris: Maspero, 1970), especially pp. 183–275. A more traditional, or at least more familiar, illustration of this critical procedure may be found in Empson's book on Milton (*Milton's God* [London: Chatto and Windus, 1961]), which can be read, in the present context, as a description of the way in which Milton's attempt to give figuration to his theology (and in particular to the "concept" of predestination) ends up, against his will, "producing" this ideology as an object for a critical or ideological (in Empson's case, essentially negative) judgment.

demonstrate its own contradictions; by the sheer formal immanence with which an ideological system exhausts its permutations and ends up projecting its own ultimate structural closure. This is, however, precisely what we will observe Wyndham Lewis' work to do; and with it, I am content to rest my case for him. However embarrassing the content of his novels may be for liberal or modernist establishment thought, it cannot but be even more painful for protofascism itself, which must thereby contemplate its own unlovely image and hear blurted out in public speech what even in private was never meant to be more than tacitly understood. Indeed, at a time when new and as yet undeveloped forms of protofascism are in the making around us, the works of Wyndham Lewis may well have acquired an all too unwanted actuality.

F. J.
August, 1978
Killingworth, Connecticut

I /
"HAIRY, SURGICAL, AND YET INVISIBLE"

> They were there in a confused mass before him. The thought of "settling everything before he went" now appeared fantastic. He had at all events started these local monsters and demons, fishing them out stark where they could be seen. Each had a different vocal explosiveness or murmur, inveighing unintelligibly against the other. The only thing to be done was to herd them all together, and march them away for inspection at leisure. Sudden herdsman, with the care of an antediluvian flock. . . .
>
> *Tarr*

O FACE THE SENTENCES OF WYNDHAM Lewis is to find oneself confronted with a principle of immense mechanical energy. Flaubert, *Ulysses*, are composed; the voices of a James or of a Faulkner develop their resources through some patient blind groping exploration of their personal idiosyncrasies from work to work. The style of Lewis, however, equally unmistakable, blasts through the tissues of his novels like a steam whistle, breaking them to its will.

For the mechanical, the machinelike, knows an exaltation peculiarly its own: "a motor-car roaring at full speed, as though bearing down upon the machine-gun itself, is more beautiful than the *Victory of Samothrace*," cried Marinetti, in words that echoed around the world like the pulsing telegraph waves upon the emblematic globe of the old newsreels, words that seem to furnish the program for

the *scène-à-faire* of Lewis' finest single novel. But for
Lewis, as for so many others, Marinetti's Futurism had
the liberating effect of a mere slogan, a static and external
caricature of what the new twentieth-century linguistic apparatus ought to register. For Lewis himself, indeed, there
could be no question of opposing nature, or the organic, to
the machine:

> Every living form is a miraculous mechanism . . .
> and every sanguinary, vicious and twisted need pro-
> duces in Nature's workshops a series of mechanical
> arrangements extremely suggestive and interesting
> for the engineer, and almost invariably beautiful or
> interesting for the artist. (*SH*, 249)

Nature itself as machine: such is the force of the
preeminently typical opening page of one of Lewis' first
great narratives, the (then) scandalous *Cantleman's Spring
Mate* of 1917:

> Cantleman walked in the strenuous fields, steam rising
> from them as though from an exertion, dissecting the
> daisies specked in the small wood, the primroses on
> the banks, the marshy lakes, and all God's creatures.
> The heat of a heavy premature Summer was cooking
> the little narrow belt of earth-air, causing everything
> innocently to burst its skin, bask abjectly and pro-
> foundly. Everything was enchanted with itself and
> with everything else. The horses considered the
> mares immensely appetizing masses of quivering
> shiny flesh: was there not something of a 'je ne sais
> quoi' about a mare, that no other beast's better-half
> possessed? (*SH*, 106)

So also for the sexual stimulation of birds, of sows and
hogs, indeed of the very human animal itself, the primor-
dial awakening of spring proving on closer inspection to
be nothing but the effect of some terrific atmospheric
pressure-cookery.

Yet this alarming demystification of the organic is conveyed in a paradoxical way: nothing is more characteristic
of Lewis' style than the peculiar rotation of our inferential

system around the adjective "strenuous"; than the peculiar slippage of the properties thus named from their official referent in the sentence. The fields, we tell ourselves, can in no case really be thought of as "strenuous": what is strenuous is at best the walk through them, or Cantleman's own exertions. Anthropomorphic projection seems an inadequate term for this shift, which classical rhetoric designated as *hypallage,* and in which "the adjective is grammatically referred to a different substantive in the context than that to which it ought semantically to be applied."[1] This minor figure of an essentially oratorical practice of language in the classical world most often stands as the sign of epic concision: we will see later that this distant affinity with Lewis' modernism is not fortuitous. Yet the classical figure is profoundly modified when, displaced, it comes to constitute the tropological infrastructure for a properly modernist practice of *style.*[2] The alternate, purely negative, designation of a *mixtura verborum* testifies to the malaise of the rhetorical episteme as it registers such anomalous phenomena that threaten to explode its limits altogether. Lewis' hypallage, where the attributes of actor or act are transferred onto the dead scenery, generates a kind of contamination of the axis of contiguity, offering a glimpse of a world in which the old-fashioned substances, like marbles in a box, have been rattled so furiously together that their "properties" come loose and stick to the wrong places—a very delirium of metonymy of which, as we shall see, Lewis' subsequent writings provide some stunning examples.

1. Heinrich Lausberg, *Elementi di retorica* (Bologna: il Mulino, 1969), p. 169.
2. On the use of the distinction between rhetoric and style as a historical and periodizing concept, see Roland Barthes, *Writing Degree Zero,* translated by Annette Lavers and Colin Smith (London: Jonathan Cape, 1967), pp. 10–13, 41–52. The distinction is that evoked by Genette, following Lubbock's differentiation between *picture* (or "report") and *scene,* as "the opposition between classical *abstraction* . . . and 'modern' *expressivity*" (Gérard Genette, *Figures* III [Paris: Seuil, 1972], p. 131); and see Percy Lubbock, *The Craft of Fiction* (New York: Viking, 1957), especially pp. 251–254.

Yet this transfer of adjectives is only the first moment of a far more complicated figural operation. No sooner do we register it, than it is itself withdrawn, undone, quite unexpectedly reversed, as though by the insertion of some new and unforeseeably more literal meaning beneath the first and figural one. It turns out, in this second moment or reversal, that Cantleman himself was nothing but a blind. Now the fields really are "strenuous" after all in their own right: overworked agents, they throw themselves enthusiastically into the business of giving off steam, perspiring from the effort of the summer's thermal preparations. Thus, what had on the story's literal level been a figure (the fields as the place of Cantleman's strenuous walk) has now, on the figural level of what the fields in spring are really like, been taken all too literally. Nor does the process stop there, for the metaphorical steam from Nature's kitchen then just as unexpectedly turns back into the steamy sweating surface of the flanks of "real" mares. Thus at length a veritable self-generating image- and sentence-producing machine comes into view behind the dextrous and imperceptible substitutions of literal and figural levels for one another.

From a somewhat different angle, we evidently have here to do with what in Roman Jakobson's influential distinction would be described as the substitution of a metaphor for a metonymy—with a metonymic figure subsequently transformed as though by sleight of hand into the complicated metaphor of nature as a single vast machine. Better still, since the spell of the initial metonymic gesture is finally never fully overcome, we have to do with a metaphoric process *concealed* behind the external trappings of a metonymic transfer; with a metaphor which can apparently emerge only disguised as metonymy; or, conversely, with an analytic, additive, mechanistic, essentially metonymic surface movement secretly powered by the natural energy of metaphoric creation. Meanwhile, if the figures themselves (metaphor/metonymy) are identified with the content of the passage (organism/machine), then it becomes clear that the passage is *autoreferential*, that is, that it laterally and unintentionally reflects back its own process of production and is in that sense "about" itself. Indeed, the entire text of this early story, which collapses sex and war or aggressivity—the organic and the machine—together into a single "ruse of Nature," can in this respect be read as a projection of the process of representation itself, or in other words, of the unnatural or artificial redoubling of "nature" by its expression, or by Language.

What is achieved by this peculiar linguistic substitution is thus essentially a demystification of the process of creation itself, an implicit repudiation of that valorization of metaphor, from Aristotle to Proust, as the "hallmark of genius," a fundamental subversion of that still organic aesthetic ideology for which the very essence of the poetic process consists in the perception, or better still, the invention, of analogies. No doubt the primacy of metaphor is the projection of a literary hierarchy for which poetry and poetic inspiration are felt to be loftier and more noble than the humdrum referential activity of prose. As Jakobson has pointed out, in an influential passage, the fundamental mechanism of realistic prose is in fact not metaphor, but metonymy:

> Following the path of contiguous relationships, the realistic author metonymically digresses from the plot to the atmosphere and from the characters to the setting in space and time. He is fond of synecdochic details. In the scene of Anna Karenina's suicide Tolstoy's artistic attention is focussed on the heroine's handbag; and in *War and Peace* the synecdoches 'hair on the upper lip' or 'bare shoulders' are used by the same writer to stand for the female characters to whom these features belong.[3]

3. Roman Jakobson and Morris Halle, *Fundamentals of Language* (The Hague: Mouton, 1956), p. 78.

In Lewis, however, metonymy is read against metaphor, as its determinate negation: it thus becomes a sign of the devaluation of inspiration itself and of the art-sentence as a composed, subjectively ripe melodic unit in its own right. We have already suggested in our Prologue that in this respect the aggressive deconstruction of metaphor and the organic in Lewis can be seen as an anticipation of the poststructuralist assault on the Romantic valorization of organic form and the symbol. Indeed, three other features of Lewis' work about which we will have something to say shortly—his conception of the subject, his attack on the phenomenological view of time, and his practice of allegory—echo and reinforce this anti-Romantic stance on other levels than the purely stylistic one. Yet in his own social context, and in the codes of the period, this figural gesture would seem to have class, rather than theoretical, connotations. Lewis' futurism thus projects the symbolic value of an antitranscendental, essentially democratic option—the machine as against the luxury furnishings of the great estates, with their ideology of natural beauty, the sheer production of sentences as against the mysteries of poetic creation and the organic primacy of the beautiful or the masterpiece.

Politically, of course, Lewis was an elitist, committed to the great man theory of history and to the defense of "intelligence" in the face of the rising tide of mass mediocrity. What we have shown about the inner logic of his stylistic practice, however, allows us to detect, in some first anticipatory way, a fundamental contradiction in this work dramatized by a practice of "textual productivity" which stands in uneasy tension with Lewis' overt or official political positions. In protofascism this tension takes the form of a rivalry between "socialist" and "nationalist" impulses, between the initial populist and anticapitalist thrust of the early fascisms, and their later vocation to secure the continuing privileges of the threatened middle-class and petty-bourgeois subject.

Yet this coexistence is itself dramatized by the dynamics of the production of Lewis' style, which is clearly a more complicated operation than the simple substitution of metonymy for metaphor, or indeed, the return to the "realistic" prose of Bennett or Wells and the outright repudiation of *fin de siècle* art language. The metaphoric content must itself be given in the text, in order to be cancelled: it is thus an initial figural richness which in some second "moment" is immediately restructured into metonymic forms and surfaces which anyone could make up for himself. Nowhere is this clearer than in those idling passages where the voice of metaphor remains silent, and metonymy functions on its own, motor wide open, in a kind of sheerly additive sentence production as accessible to the "common man" as carpentry or literacy itself.

In such purely metonymic passages, the machine in Lewis' style generates a whole painstaking and analytic dismemberment of the external world and of gesture, a kind of tireless visual inventory which reminds us of nothing so much as the more famous bravura or antibravura descriptions of *Tristram Shandy,* and with which, given some initial object of representation, page upon page might effortlessly be filled:

> Don Alvaro could not have moved more slowly off the table had he been demonstrating the exercise to a slow-witted beginner in gymnastics: first he uncrossed his legs with a languourous slowness that suspended the leg he was thus translating for an appreciable accretion of seconds in mid-air; and he dropped it down beside the other with as much deliberation—as much inch by inch—as if the floor which was to receive it had been a hot brick, or an uncomfortable icicle. (*RL*, 15)

This step-by-step dismantling of the body's gestural machine implies that reality is itself infinitely divisible, that its smallest atomic units can themselves be further and further subdivided by an infinitely expandable accretion of sentences, towards some unimaginable infinitesimality.

And like the body, the mind can be conceived as a mechanism also, which at its worst reproduces itself in the same additive fashion:

> Pulley has been most terribly helpful and kind there's no excusing himself Pulley has been most terribly helpful and kind—most terribly helpful and he's been kind. He's been most terribly kind and helpful, there are two things, he's been most kind he's been terribly helpful, he's kind he can't help being—he's terribly. (*CM*, 44)

This mindless babble is of course designed to represent what Lewis thought of as the gertrude "steining" of the modern child cult. Yet like the external anatomies, it projects a notion of the object as something decomposable ad infinitum, before which the writer places himself like a draughtsman, prepared to blacken "tireless" pages in frightening quantities. *The Apes of God* is indeed a kind of ambiguous monument to this illimitable sentence-producing capacity, which is itself a figure for human productive power in the industrial age.

It is therefore not surprising to find immense arid stretches in Lewis' often hastily composed works which are a deliberate provocation of the reader fully as much as they challenge a ritualistic cult of *belles lettres* or high style. Paradoxically, however, such "flaws," such sloppy writing, only confirm the immense and liberating energies of Lewis' style; for in such passages the principle of sheer sentence production is foregrounded and separates itself off as a now dominant force in its own right from all the individual sentences it leaves strewn behind it. The sentences of Joyce are composed according to a principle of immanence, God withdrawing from view behind his creation: in Lewis, however, sheer proliferation stands as the sign and ratification of his mechanistic enterprise.

In practice, of course, limits are placed on this infinite generation of empty sentences: from a contemporary standpoint, we would say that the textual impulse in Lewis is then strategically recontained by various devices, of which we will examine the narrative ones in our next chapter. But even the theoretical awareness of this production is carefully held in check: such is, for example, the function of a certain scientistic bias which presides over the systematic analysis and disjunction of the metonymic pole. "Burying Euclid deep in the living flesh,"[4] his characterization of the central impulse of his painting, was surely in his mind the motto for his linguistic practice as well.

Yet in the present day and age, in which scientific research has come to be understood as the construction of models, we are perhaps less intimidated by such invocations of the scientific absolute. From a stylistic point of view, even this scientific component of Lewis' language can be viewed as a single code or vocabulary field, a single terminological stock, among many other, equally distinctive, equally unprivileged sublanguages: the deliberately flourished anglicisms and British colloquialisms, for example ("fuss," "toddle," "beastly," "strapping"); or yet again the explicitly "painterly" and technical signals in certain descriptive passages, as though carefully blocked off by the expert's thumb extended to full distance.

The point to be made about these subcodes or idiolects is not their hierarchy but rather their sheer multiplicity, their jealously respected inconsistency with one another. No effort is made to fuse them into some more personal unity of tone. On the contrary, their very function is to interfere with each other, to clash visibly within the sentence itself in such a way that no surface homogeneity has time to reform: the words, unable to go together properly, end up projecting the warring planes and angles of a cubist painting. The sentence is thus an amalgam of heterogeneous forces which must not be allowed to congeal. Hence the ultimate and ineducable unruliness of the Lewis

---

4. Quoted in Walter Michel, ed., *Wyndham Lewis: Paintings and Drawings* (Berkeley and Los Angeles: University of California Press, 1971), p. 40.

style, half-baked by design, and structurally too scandalous even for the most accommodating Pantheon, as, emblematically, in his well-known description of the Trolls ("hairy, surgical, and yet invisible"). That the composition of such sentences is a visual process, a juxtaposition and collage of word-objects felt to possess well-nigh tangible properties, may be judged from the effects of Lewis' blindness: unlike Joyce, the Lewis of the final years, able only to think or hear his language, reverts to an almost eighteenth-century sobriety, the fireworks of the earlier style now passing over into the content of the narratives themselves.

2/
AGONS OF THE
PSEUDO-COUPLE

I have described the nature of my own humour—how,
as I said, it went over into everything, making a drama
of mock-violence of every social relationship. Why
should it be so *violent*—so mock-violent—you may at
the time have been disposed to enquire? Everywhere it
has seemed to be compelled to go into some frame that
was always a simulacrum of mortal combat.

The Wild Body

HE APPARENTLY INDETERMINABLE CA-
pacity of the sentence-producing mech-
anism, the random fission of the metonymic impulse, cannot, however, be
permitted to operate unchecked. Pro-
liferating according to their own inner
logic, the accumulation of molecular sentences threatens to
deposit vast sheets of surface decoration and to smooth the
most violent agitation of detail back over into a static and
well-nigh visual frieze, into some dizzying churrigueresque
cramming of all the empty spaces. At its outer limit, then,
even the flat surface and the discipline of the visual might
be expected to be undermined, exploding the conventions
and strategies of classical modernism and generating the
openly schizophrenic discontinuities of such postmodernist
"texts" or *écriture* as Beckett's *Watt*. The mode of Lewis'
verbal production, however, remains narrative, rather than
lyrical or schizophrenic. We must therefore now show how

the energies of the metonymic, how the molecular vio-
lences of Lewis' individual sentences, are recontained and
checked, diverted and recontrolled, by some external principle of reunification, by that countercompulsion of abstract unity and empty global closure which—in distinction
to their concept of the molecular—Deleuze and Guattari
have conveniently termed the "molar."

It is in fact the painterly relationship, the situation of
the artist-writer before his model, which gives the first clue
as to the structure of such molar recontainment. No one is
better placed than the draughtsman to sense the exchange
of forces generated between the observer's point of view
and the object contemplated, between the model and the
eye that takes its inventory. Nor is this some static cogni-
tive union of the knower with the known, but rather at
once reorganizes itself into two mechanisms squaring off
against each other, each quasi-automatically readjusting itself to the automatic movements and tremors of its opposite number, as in that moment in *The Childermass* in
which the zombielike longshoreman poles his boat over
against the figure (Pullman) gazing back at him from the
bank:

> A stone's-throw out he stops, faces the shore, study-
> ing sombrely in perspective the man-sparrow, who
> multiplies precise movements, an organism which in
> place of speech has evolved a peripatetic system
> of response to a dead environment. It has wandered
> beside this Styx, a lost automaton rather than a lost
> soul. . . . (*C*, 11)

Man-machine responding to dead environment, automata
in specular reaction to each other: such is the protonarra-
tive form generated from out of that seemingly contemplative stance of the detached observer which characterized
the title figure of *Tarr* and the narrator of *The Wild Body*,
not to speak of the painter Lewis himself. We now need to
understand how the production of narrative in Lewis'
novels is both enabled and strategically recontained by this

primal relationship, this reciprocal interaction of tics and twitches ordered into an obligatory circuit, a reflex of vaso-motor action and reaction which provides the spectacle of a ceaseless exchange of sparks between any two existents felt as contrary or opposing poles.

Ultimately, of course, such sparks will take the form of speech itself, words and voices hotly flung down as trumps of one another. This is the exemplary value of the Bailiff's reaction to the intervention of his primal adversary, Hyperides:

> electrified at the impact of the new voice . . . he lights up all over. The sounds stagger his senses like a salvo from a gong announcing battle from the positions of a legendary enemy. It is a hail from the contrary pole, it opens for him by magic the universe that lies between which before the voice came was closed and dead. (*C*, 152–153)

Dialogue is too weak a term for such exchanges, which, in their violent *stichomythia,* define a veritable *agon* between the polar adversaries. This is the very element of Lewis' novelistic world, this combative, exasperated, yet jaunty stance of monads in collision, a kind of buoyant truculence in which matched and abrasive consciousnesses slowly rub each other into smarting vitality.

Such a conception of human relationships explains why for Lewis, who saw his privileged role as the essentially nonsocial one of artist or pure eye, the most desirable condition of human existence remains that of solitude. Thus the doomed lovers of *The Revenge for Love* wish for nothing better than to be left alone by their insistent contemporaries; while the aging Lewis himself, longing for a world stilled of the conflicts of the political and of political parties, conceived some ultimate vision of the peace of divine and angelic *indifference.*

This is the sense in which the opening scene of *Tarr* stages that revulsion with the social, that symptomatic hesitation and reluctance in the face of the most insignificant human contacts, against the unpropitious background of which all the later dramatic and explosive conflicts in Lewis will take place:

> Hobson and Tarr met in the Boulevard du Paradis.
> —They met in a gingerly, shuffling fashion: they
> had so many good reasons for not slowing down
> when they met, numbers of antecedent meetings
> when it would have been better if they had kept on,
> all pointing to *why* they *should* crush their hats down
> over their eyes and hurry forward, so that it was a
> defeat and unsanitary to have their bodies shuffling
> and gesticulating there. (*T*, 9–10)

Under such circumstances, all human relations are bound to have something vaguely ominous about them; and the more heightened moments of scandal or violence prove to be nothing but the convulsive effort to free one's self from one's interlocutor, or—as with the fearful Kreisler—to obliterate him in an explosion of rage and black bile.

Lewis thus takes a unique and original place in that distinctive subtradition of the modern novel which may be termed the interpersonal or dialogical narrative.[1] This subtradition must of course be understood in terms of the general situation of modernism as a whole, for which some older common-sense notion of "reality" has become problematical, and with it, a traditional faith in the transparency of language and an unselfconscious practice of mimetic representation, along with the very categories of experience and events themselves (what Barthes will call, as we shall see in a moment, the proairetic code). Now all the concrete determinations of the older social novel—the empirical detail of everyday life, the insertions of class or of the industrial city, the slow fashion- or furniture-change of the decades, the material coordinates of workplace or mechanical conveyance, of technological marvel or of political institutions—are felt as so much contingent matter,

---

1. The term is Mikhail Bakhtin's. See *Problems of Dostoevski's Poetics*, translated by R. W. Rotsel (Ann Arbor: Ardis, 1973), pp. 150–169.

not be welcomed lavishly as into the abundant descriptions of the older realism, but eyed with all the suspicion of a foreign body, of the inert resistance of matter to the newly autonomous realm of aesthetic language. The modernist gesture is thus ideological and Utopian all at once: perpetuating the increasing subjectivization of individual experience and the atomization and disintegration of the older social communities, expressing the anxiety and revulsion of intellectuals before the reification of social life and the ever intensifying class conflicts of industrial society, it also embodies a will to overcome the commodification of late nineteenth-century capitalism, and to substitute for the mouldering and overstuffed bazaar of late Victorian life the mystique and promise of some intense and heightened, more authentic existence.

To take inventory of the various possible symbolic reactions to this situation would involve an anatomy of modernism in all the ranges of its stylization, from efforts to transcend reason and logic, as hostages of a degraded culture or reality-principle, all the way to the attempt to extirpate matter as such and to make language the space for some pure and liberated play of spirit beyond contingency. As far as the novel is concerned, the most influential modernist strategy is surely that marked by the "discovery" of the interior monologue and organized around the exploration of individual consciousness and its unconscious from the inside, around the verbal "rendering" of the inner reality of the monad which amounts in fact to a veritable production of the latter, and of contemporary subjectivity, as though for the first time.[2]

It is from such subjectivizing and impressionistic, often sheerly solipsistic, forms that we must learn to distinguish the rather different strategy of the dialogical tradition. The latter aims no less at a repression of its concrete situational

---

2. The classical statement of this properly impressionistic aesthetic is Harry Levin, *James Joyce* (Norfolk, Ct.: New Directions, 1941). Lewis explicitly took this book as a polemic coordinate in *Men Without Art*.

determinations, at a transmutation of contingency, than the former; yet its cult is one of relationship rather than of individual experience and intensity. Where hegemonic modernism finds its ultimate ground in the body itself and everything inexpressible in the physiological infrastructure of the monad, this countertrend strikes out in the direction of the collective, which however it strategically recontains, freezing it over and reifying it in the mirage of what is today widely termed "intersubjectivity." The ill-assorted exemplars of this new and fragmentary tendency would number such writers as Lewis' contemporary, D. H. Lawrence; or those Russian novelists from Dostoyevsky to Olesha whose passionate intermonadic dialogues struggle to overcome a characteristic inner sense of grotesqueness, an endemic ego-deficiency or identity failure, which, virtually a Russian literary tradition, resulted from the backwardness of the Russian bourgeoisie; and it would surely include those French novels of our own period which, under the galvanic shock of Sartre's discovery of the Look as the privileged form of our alienation by the Other, have sought to project new visions of the dialogical level of social life in the varying modes of Simone de Beauvoir's *L'Invitée (She Came to Stay)*; of the elliptical and ritualistic communions of Marguerite Duras; and of Nathalie Sarraute's sense of human relations as the virtually instinctive tremors of organic tropisms.

It is indeed Nathalie Sarraute who, with her conception of the "subconversation" has perhaps best—long after the fact—defined the structure of the kind of narrative in question here. Her slogan designates and presupposes a situation in which the apparent surface conversation is no longer the real one; in which, beneath the routine and insignificant, contingent exchange of spoken words, there comes into view some more fundamental human contact, some deeper wordless groping struggle or interaction. It is as though the old common language of everyday life had ceased to be an adequate vehicle for individual expression, let alone communication. Brittle with cliché, great surfaces of it corroded by publicity and received ideas, that alienated and conventionalized language begins to break apart, leaving deserts of silence visible between the cracks. Here genuine human life continues to exist, but as it were underground, beneath the dead surface of social routine and convention. The task of the novelist then becomes the recuperation of that more authentic reality and the invention of a new and fresh, nonalienated, *originary* language in which the latter's preverbal or nonverbal events and incidents can somehow, beyond all fallen speech, be adequately rendered.

An aesthetic of this kind inevitably proposes a kind of "double articulation" or surcharged text—a text and commentary structure within the text itself—whose stylistic consequences will be examined in the next chapter. What must concern us here is the effect of the new relational or dialogical form on those traditional categories of object, event, and character which secured the representational surface of the older unselfconscious realisms. These unreflected categories of a common-sense view of "reality" are now powerfully displaced by the new scaffolding of the agon, whose rigid polarization in its turn releases the variables in any given relationship to an unaccustomed and properly expressionist mutability. It is as though the stable substances of Aristotelian science, with their fixed and describable properties, were suddenly projected into the relational fields of post-Einsteinian physics, and, as in a Gestalt reversal, transformed into the termini or poles of a relationship which now defines and takes logical priority over them. Their various determinations can thus be modified at will, provided that both poles vary in correlation with each other: nor can the kinship with the contemporary linguistic doctrine of the binary opposition be overlooked, of which Saussure observed that in it "there are only differences *without positive terms.*"[3]

3. Ferdinand de Saussure, *Course in General Linguistics*, translated by Wade Baskin (New York: McGraw Hill, 1966), p. 120.

The most immediate and striking symptoms of this new narrative structure will thus be the ceaseless metamorphosis of its object world. The relational perspective of the new dialogical system explicitly suppresses the contingency of the material backdrop or setting within which such relationships might be supposed to play themselves out. Yet the objects do not for all that disappear, even where no place analogous to older realistic description has been foreseen for them. On the contrary, Lewis was in some deep Bachelardian fashion haunted his whole life long by rooms and houses, by dwelling space as such. The mystery of these material structures seems to intensify in dialectical proportion to the degree to which the struggle between subjects and subject-poles is emphasized, as though the incomprehensible requirement for people to come together within walled boxes of various sizes and thicknesses became the occasion for a quasi-existential reflection of the narrative upon its own structural limits.[4]

In early Lewis, then, the obsession with rooms and buildings stands as a kind of "return of the repressed" of contingent and material content, which now tends to reinsert itself in anthropomorphic form into the place of one of the subject poles of the agon. Now rooms and houses come to live the momentary life of a minor and episodic character, making appearances in which, as in the following "biographical sketch" of a popular Parisian eating place in *Tarr*, a whole organic life-process, as in time-lapse cinematography, is speeded up before the reader's eye:

> The Restaurant Vallet, like many of its neighbours,
> had been originally a clean tranquil little creamery,

4. *Monstre gai* enlarges this fascination into the systematic exploration of a whole city (Third City, or "the Magnetic City"), thereby reinventing in narrative form the discursive and explanatory segments of the classical Utopia. The generic cross-reference for *The Childermass* (particularly its first half) would however be so-called New Wave science fiction, particularly hallucinogenic narratives like Brian Aldiss' *Barefoot in the Head* (New York: Ace, 1969). And see for a discussion of Lewis' fascination with rooms, as well as for a stylistic analysis quite different from the one offered here, John Russell, *Style in Modern British Fiction* (Baltimore: Johns Hopkins University Press, 1978), pp. 123–157.

consisting of a small shop a few feet either way. Then
one after another its customers had lost their reserve:
they had asked, in addition to their daily glass of
milk, for côtes de pré salé and similar massive
nourishment, which the decent little business at first
supplied with timid protest. But perpetual scenes of
unbridled voracity, semesters of compliance with the
most brutal appetites of man, gradually brought
about a change in its character; it became frankly a
place where the most full-blooded palate might be
satisfied. As trade grew the small business had
burrowed backwards into the ramshackle house:
bursting through walls and partitions, flinging down
doors, it discovered many dingy rooms in the interior
that it hurriedly packed with serried cohorts of eat-
ers. It had driven out terrified families, had hemmed
the apoplectic concierge in her 'loge', it had broken
out on to the court at the back in shed-like
structures: and in the musty bowels of the house it
had established a broiling luridly lighted roaring den,
inhabited by a fierce band of slatternly savages.

(*T*, 87–88)

The ferocity with which this 'decent little business' is de-
praved and corrupted by the carnivorous demands of its
clients recapitulates the reciprocal interaction of the agon
and gives us, at the same time, a first hint of the violence
and aggressivity immanent in this structure.

But the sketch of the Restaurant Vallet is a bravura
piece: normally such objects must range themselves within
the longer-term narrative struggles of the novel, speaking
languages of their own to which the novelist must give new
voice, just as he must reinvent the unspoken language of
the subconversation of its "human" characters. Thus another room, Bertha's, momentarily substituting for the latter in Tarr's agon with her, comes to emit its own characteristic note, "cheap and dead, but rich with the same
lifelessness as the trees without" (*T*, 44); while later on

the abject little room seemed to be thrust forward to
awaken his memories and ask for pity. An intense
atmosphere of teutonic suicide permeated everything;

> he could not move an eyelid or a muscle without
> wounding or slighting something: it was like being in
> a dark kitchen at night, where you know at every
> step you will put your foot upon a beetle. . . .
>
> (*T*, 289)

Such an entity as this room has clearly become a momentary *actant*, a surrogate for the heroine herself, something on the order of the more ignoble Racinian *confidentes*. Such a narrative component is neither symbol nor "impression": too stubbornly active to be a mere phenomenological rendering of Tarr's experience of his object world, it is also too intermittent, too punctual in time, too fully an event, to project any stable symbolism.

Nor are human bodies themselves any more resistant to this powerful restructuration: as with the metonymic fission of its acts and gestures, the body now fragments into hosts of objects which can be foregrounded in their turn, even though, given their conventionally "expressive" functions, they tend to be rebuked by a presentation that shows them to be, if anything, even less articulate than the surrounding landscape:

> The over flesh-coloured face (as if violently pretend-
> ing to be flesh and blood at all costs) with the
> preposterous false bottom to it gazed at the portrait.
> It gazed and gazed with a cowlike, cud-chewing con-
> centration. All the irritability of the last fortnight or
> more of suspense smouldered in the capacious false
> bottom of this fauxbonhomme's headpiece—with its
> leaden secretions it weighed down this impossibly in-
> nocent chin. For it could be a receptacle on occasion
> for dissatisfaction, as well as for bluff 'kindliness'.
> The complete gamut of hatred felt by its owner for
> this disaffected craftsman expressed itself in the
> expressionless eyes, as their vacuity deepened from
> blankness to abysses of utter blankness, from a bland
> blankness to a brutish blankness, from Pickwick or
> Pecksniff to the orang-outang: till nature's dark
> abhorrence of a vacuum—of such a vacuum!—
> became so intolerable as to be really malignant.
>
> (*RL*, 232)

In such a world, a world of fragments reorganized into active, anthropomorphic entities, an intermittent chaos of messages from all angles of space, an intolerable solicitation of shifting subinvolvements into which we are plunged up to the eyes—in such a world the very nature of the *event* must be transformed beyond recognition.

In this reality, as blurred as a hand held up before the face, only movement signals the operation of events themselves and allows us to detect the presence of the exchange of forces characteristic of the Lewis agon:

> 'Oh dis—m'aimes-tu? Dis que tu m'aimes!' A blurting, hurrying personality rushed right up into his face. He was very familiar with it. It was like the sightless clammy charging of a bat. Humbug had temptestuously departed: their hot-house was suffering a blast of outside air. He stared at her face groping up as though it scented mammals in his face: it pushed to right, then to left, and rocked itself.
>
> (*T*, 51)

More is at stake in such passages than that "estrangement" of the habitual which is characteristic of so many modernisms. There is, to be sure, an initial moment of this reading operation (to which we will return in the next chapter), in which the *name* that such peculiar nuzzlement bears in the common-sense proairetic code of everyday reality (we call it an *embrace*, a *buss*, a *kiss*)[5] must be rees-

---

5. See Roland Barthes, *S/Z*, translated by Richard Miller (New York: Hill and Wang, 1974):

> "What is a series of actions? the unfolding of a name. To *enter*? I can unfold it into 'to appear' and 'to penetrate'. To *leave*? I can unfold it into 'to want to', 'to stop', 'to leave again'. To *give*?: 'to incite', 'to return', 'to accept'. Inversely, to establish the sequence is to find the name." (82) "The proairetic sequences. . . . are born of a certain power of the reading, which tries to give a sufficiently transcendent name to a series of actions, themselves deriving from a patrimonial hoard of human experiences. . . . The typology of these proaireticisms seems uncertain or . . . at least they can be assigned no logic other than that of the probable, of empirics, of the 'already-done' or 'already-written', for the number and the order of their terms vary, some deriving from a practical reservoir of trivial everyday acts. . . . and others from a written corpus of novelistic models." (203–204)

tablished, allowing us to measure the force of the stylization or the estrangement.

But the older and more familiar event does not return
unchanged: from the stereotypical categories of Barthes'
proairetic code (walking, talking, opening doors, eating,
feeling annoyance, embracing, envying, turning away,
rushing forward)—molar unities of a traditional kind
which are surely present in the oldest languages with
which we are familiar—the event has now been systematically rewritten into a new, more global, and less familiar
molar unity, in which it comes before us as a duel, a struggle, a contest of every instant, a situation of strategic and
tactical embattlement in which one can make the right or
the wrong move. Thus Bertha, planning the proper explanation for her scandalous public embrace of the disreputa-
ble Kreisler, must plot out her strategy:

> Her account of things could not of course be blurted
> out, it had to grow out of circumstances. Indeed as
> long a time as possible must be allowed to elapse be-
> fore she referred to it directly. It must almost seem as
> though she were going to say nothing; impressive
> silence—nothing. Their minds, accustomed to her si-
> lence, would, when it came, find the explanation all
> the more impressive. (*T*, 157–158)

Unfortunately, in such a situation, in which one's gestures
and one's very silences are mobilized and organized by
larger strategic concepts, one can also be outflanked: these
are battles one can also lose, when trumped by a superior
opponent. Thus Fräulein Liepman, in a shrewd and instinctive countermove, dismisses Kreisler as unworthy of
any further comment, thus cutting the ground from beneath her adversary's plan:

> Bertha's story had come uncomfortably and difficultly
> to flower. No one seemed to want to hear it. She
> wished she had not waited so long. But, the matter
> put in the light given it by Fräulein Liepman, she
> must not delay: she was, there was no question about
> it, in some sense responsible for Kreisler. It was her

duty to *explain* him: but now Fräulein Liepman had
put an embargo on explanations: there were to be no
more explanations. The subject was drawing peril-
ously near the point where it would be dropped. . . .
(*T*, 159)

It is instructive to compare such scenes with the analogous
Proustian anatomy of the malicious dynamism of social
life. Proust's account of such painful snubs and *gaffes*,
and of their eager exploitation by our interlocutors, tends,
through the retrospective character of his impressionistic
narrative, to reorient their anecdotal force in the direction
of a metaphysical thesis about human nature (the intolerable and unsatisfying character of life in society in general, and of human relationships in particular, against
which the supreme value of the solitary practice of aesthetic re-creation disengages itself).

Lewis' relational universe has no place for a thesis
about human nature, as we shall see more clearly when we
come to consider the status of the individual subject in it.
If thesis there is, then we have here rather to do with a
narrative presupposition about the structure of events, as
moments in which subjects come into painful, fitful and
undesirable contacts with one another; and this structure
reaches down into the most minimal encounters of a space
and time as packed as an egg. In such space there is no
longer any narrative perspective: background such as
Kreisler's financial situation, which would normally be rel-
egated to an exposition that prepared this or that scene, is
now laid out on the surface of the text along with the
major crises, and Kreisler's relationship to his friend Ernst
Vokt is foregrounded beyond any casual link of borrower
to borrowee: "He was now in a position analogous to that
of a man who had been separated for some months from
his wife: he was in a luxurious hurry once more to see the
colour of Vokt's gold" (*T*, 78). With this inflection, an
inert fact about Kreisler, a static detail in his complicated
life situation, becomes a field of force in which other events

can in turn be generated. For one thing, Kreisler discovers
that something has changed in their "relationship"; bor-
rowing is no longer so effortless or matter-of-fact an activity:

> It was only gradually that he realized of how much
> more value Vokt's money now was, and what before
> was an unorganized mass of specie, in which the pro-
> fessional borrower could wallow, was now a sound
> and suitably conducted business. (*T*, 80)

At length, the nascent situation generates a new and unexpected counterforce; "Vokt" is reorganized into a battle-
field across which Kreisler advances to meet a hitherto unknown enemy:

> Louis Soltyk was a young Russian Pole, who occa-
> sionally sat amongst the Germans at the Berne; and
> of him Vokt saw more than of anybody; in fact it was
> he who had superseded Kreisler in the position of
> influence as regards Vokt's purse. But Soltyk did not
> borrow a hundred marks: his system was far more up
> to date. Ernst had experienced an unpleasant shock
> in coming into contact with Kreisler's clumsy and
> slovenly money habits again. (*T*, 81)

So at length the agon reemerges fully-blown out of the
most minimal narrative pretexts. Nor is its function exhausted by this account of the obsessively conflictual organization of Lewis' world. On the contrary, as we shall show
in a later section, thus restructured, thus preprepared,
the "event" may now be considered an "apparatus" capable of being invested with all kinds of supplementary
meanings, both instinctual and national-political: in the
present passage, for example, it will be a matter of no
small consequence that the collision between Kreisler's
"method" and Soltyk's is evoked in terms of the shock
between lower and higher cultures.

We have already begun to appreciate to what degree
the relational reorganization of narrative in Lewis compels
a fundamental transformation in the basic tokens, the

categories and building blocks, with which plot is traditionally constructed. The discovery is of course one we have already made in other contexts: half a century of stylized abstraction in all the media, Freud's demonstration of the inner logic of dreams, Lévi-Strauss' analysis of *pensée sauvage*, the narrative models of Propp and Greimas, have all in their various ways reinforced the proposition that narrative is a purely temporal form whose content is relatively indifferent; that it is not the substance and the intrinsic interest of actors or objects which determines narrative power, but rather quite the reverse, that a powerful narrative structure generates its own specific "bearers" and tokens, its own components and terms. For the dreaming mind, indeed, an intelligible "plot" can be fashioned out of the most heterogeneous odds and ends— the contents of a bathroom cupboard, say—which—as with Magritte's enormous combs and shaving brushes— come little by little, in their interaction, to be invested with all the meaning and the "personality" of the pieces on a chessboard. So for Tarr, Bertha's room, the bust of Beethoven, but also his own thoughts (some of them stale and obsessive, others with the insolence of a peremptory advertising slogan), nervous fingers that drum some incomprehensible but urgent message, faces like ominous buildings in which enemies lie in ambush—all come to be fitful yet significant characters in their own right.

But if this is the case, then what needs to be rethought is the very category of the literary "character" itself. Propp and Greimas took important steps in this direction, the first by attempting to rewrite characters in terms of narrative *functions*, the second by therapeutically reducing the character to the status of a support or bearer of action (the untranslatable concept of the *actant*) and showing that in strategic cases what seems to be a single unified character, held together by a proper name, can under narrative analysis be revealed as an uneasy plurality of quite distinct *actants* or functions, a structural coexistence rather than an organic substance or "identity."[6] Still, except in such exemplary structural ambiguities where the concept becomes a negative and critical instrument for demystifying an illusion of anthropomorphic representation, Greimas' *actant* remains dangerously assimilable to the conventional category of the character.[7]

Yet such reflections remain metacritical. At best, therefore, their terminology continues to designate categories at work in the analysis of all narrative, rather than specific historical modifications of narrative and character structure of the kind here under study. In the Sapir-Whorf hypothesis that for better or for worse governs the historical and social analysis of form—implying that linguistic articulation fully recapitulates the operations of consciousness; that where no specific formal category exists, or where it has disappeared, the concept governed by that category may be supposed to be absent from, or repressed in, the formal episteme of the period—we must take the problem of the literary character, and its formal modifications, as the privileged symptom of the problem of the subject itself, and its constitution or disintegration. If, in other words, we mean to be serious about that task which contemporary theory calls the "decentering" of the subject, if we want to draw the ultimate practical consequences of the current (Lacanian) view that the subject is an "effect of structure" (Lacan's extension of Freud's original program for a "Copernican Revolution" in the human studies), then

6. See Vladimir Propp, *Morphology of the Folktale*, translated by Lawrence Scott (Austin, Texas: University of Texas Press, 1968); and A. J. Greimas, *Du Sens* (Paris: Seuil, 1970), esp. "Éléments d'une grammaire narrative," and also, Greimas, "Les Actants, les Acteurs et les Figures," in Claude Chabrol, ed., *Sémiotique narrative et textuelle* (Paris: Larousse, 1973), pp. 161–176.

7. Elsewhere I have suggested that it would be desirable to ground the "character-effect" in the hypothesis of an underlying character *system*, which, like the system of proper names, generates the individual character and on which the latter's narrative meaning depends. See "Character Systems in *La Vieille Fille*," in my book, *The Political Unconscious* (Ithaca, N.Y.: Cornell University Press, forthcoming).

we must pay special attention to those forms in which the traditional representation of the subject shows signs of breaking down, in which narrative itself begins to undermine what the structuralists and poststructuralists would call the humanistic paradigm, the received idea of a preexisting human nature and the illusion of an autonomous, centered "self" or personal identity.

It is precisely the disintegration of such categories which D. H. Lawrence evokes in a famous letter in which he reflects on the deeper subversive mission of futurism:

> What is interesting in the laugh of the woman is the same as the binding of the molecules of steel or their action in heat; it is the inhuman will, call it physiology, or like Marinetti—physiology of matter, that fascinates me. I don't so much care about what the woman *feels*—in the ordinary usage of the word. That presupposes an *ego* to feel with. . . . You mustn't look in my novel for the old stable *ego* of the character. There is another *ego,* according to which the individual is unrecognisable, and passes through, as it were, allotropic states which it needs a deeper sense than any we've been used to exercise, to discover are states of the same radically unchanged element. (Like as diamond and coal are the same pure single element of carbon. The ordinary novel would trace the history of the diamond—but I say, 'Diamond, what! This is carbon.' And my diamond might be coal or soot, and my theme is carbon.)[8]

And should it be suspected that Lawrentian decentering operates more freely and joyously on the Woman-Other than on the central, and phallocentric, male consciousness, we need only jump ahead in time to the Deleuze-Guattari aesthetic, with its concept of the non- or inhuman nature of sexuality,[9] to measure the trajectory that leads from dis-

8. Letter to Edward Garnett, June 5, 1914, in *Collected Letters,* ed. Harry T. Moore (New York: Viking, 1962), I, p. 282. The entire letter is of the greatest interest.

9. Gilles Deleuze and Felix Guattari, *Anti-Oedipus: Capitalism and Schizophrenia,* translated by Robert Hurley, Mark Seem and Helen R. Lane (New

satisfaction with traditional representations of character to the overt celebration of the schizophrenic dissolution of the personality in general.

Lawrence's program for narrative, indeed, shows remarkable affinities with Lewis' own mature aesthetic, idiosyncratically conceived as *satire,* by which Lewis meant to underscore the nonethical, purely external mode of his new representation as cubist-caricatural, its materialist techniques affirming their kinship with the visual, rather than the temporal, arts, with space rather than time, and knowing a symbolic mission to discredit the shapeless warm organic *durée* of the inner monologue and of a psychology-oriented subjectivism.[10]

This aesthetic, and its consequences for the old stable subject or ego, can best be observed in the texts Lewis produced after what we will call the "break" in his work, when the relatively stable, homeostatic psychic allegory of *Tarr* can no longer function, and "reality" itself dissolves into the hallucinatory phantasmagoria of Lewis' theological science fiction, in *The Childermass.* Here, where matter is annulled, we confront the most delirious and bewildering metamorphoses of worldly space itself and of its constituent elements. With this immense overcrowding of the shores of the dead by the fearful "slaughter of the innocents" of World War I, we seem to have come as close as language can bring us to an uncontrolled experience of the schizophrenic flux: yet unlike later, more officially schizophrenic texts (Beckett's *Watt* may again serve as an

York: Viking, 1977), p. 294. The reference is to Marx, *Early Writings,* translated by Rodney Livingstone and Gregor Benton (London: Penguin, 1975), p. 156; glossed by Lyotard in *Discours, figure* (Paris: Klincksieck, 1971), pp. 138–141.

10. For Lewis' most complete statement on the aesthetic of satire, see *Men Without Art* (London: Cassell, 1934), pp. 103–128. The Lawrence letter quoted above echoes Lewis' insistence on the nonmoral thrust of this externalizing discourse: "Somehow that which is physical, non-human, in humanity, is more interesting to me than the old-fashioned human element—which causes one to conceive a character in a certain moral scheme and make him consistent. The certain moral scheme is what I object to."

exemplary point of reference), this "experience" remains locked into narrative categories and organized by narrative values.

The adventures of the novel's heroes, Pullman and Satterthwaite, among the treacherous and shifting "time flats" mark a curious compromise between the whirling flux of perpetual change into which these "characters" are drawn, and the "fourth wall" of representational observation which the reader continues to occupy. What orders this apparent flux and lends its unpredictable transformations the security of a properly narrative continuity is clearly the persistence of the relational structure, the agon form, now hypostatized in the unity of the couple itself. Whatever Pulley or Satters may turn into individually, their relationship to each other remains and provides a stable system of coordinates to which the changes may be pegged: thus Satters becomes a baby, an old man, a navvy, a cockney soldier, a vamp, and a public school boy in rapid succession; yet Pullman, altering his own age and identity to follow suit, thereby continues to perceive him as "the same": "The time- and class-scales in which they hang in reciprocal action are oscillating violently, as they rush up and down through neighbouring dimensions they sight each other only imperfectly" (*CM*, 115).

It will be observed that some of the most striking "transformations" in the opening phantasmagoria of *The Childermass* are in reality little more than expressionist intensifications of figures of speech that dramatize this or that passing attitude or reaction. Thus Pullman's protective and bossy relationship to his wayward charge emerges as the persona of Nurse Pullman, "distant and strong-minded, not-sniffing, not-offended, a tart smart tight little governess" (*CM*, 16). Yet in the world of the time-flats it is precisely this distinction between the figurative and the literal that has disappeared. In this sense, the Science Fiction convention of the novel allows Lewis' style to fulfill tendencies which must necessarily be checked by the enabling frame of a more "realistic" novel, in which the narrative line is to be taken as the "literal" level upon which the various figures are embroidered. On the other hand, the suppression of the distinction between literal and figurative language is not itself a new aesthetic, but rather a situation and a dilemma to which the various modernist aesthetics react in distinct ways, "solving" it by the production of styles and texts which constitute a host of different symbolic acts. What we have called Lewis' "expressionism," for example, may be defined as the will, in this new linguistic crisis, to transform the figurative into the literal, to kick away the metaphorical apparatus by which we have risen into the figural, and to affirm the latter as a final, if merely provisional, "reality." It is not, however, as we shall see, an uncontradictory solution (any more than those of the other modernisms).

The official subject of *The Human Age* is, of course, the personality itself and the threats the modern world holds in store for the "strong" personalities of an intelligent elite. What is clear even at the level of stylistic practice which concerns us here is that the "personalities" of Pullman and Satters are far less real than whatever is happening to them. Their transformations are a function of the situation itself; their passing attributes, literalized into real metamorphoses, are in reality mechanical adaptations to that larger transpersonal unity whose figural characterization dictates their own. The shaping power of apposition or epithet, which is the dominant stylistic device of *The Childermass,* and in terms of which its characters reappear in the varying disguises of "Ka Pullman," "Bill-Sykes-Satters," "big burning Gretchen," "the Styx-side sheikh," marks the priority of some global stereotype of these various moments over the characterization of any of its individual elements, including the subject or "character" itself.

This means that in Lewis' narrative such categories as "irony" and "point of view" are no longer relevant. When

Pullman's journey through this uncharted realm is "rendered" in sentences such as the following one:

> A veteran rat, trotting in an aerial gutter, he catches a glimpse of glittering chasms but averts his eyes . . .
>
> (*CM*, 17)

the unpleasant overtones of the new avatar remain somehow undetected by the medium, which seems to transcend the pejorative and the sympathetic equally. It is as though the whole mechanism of empathy and ethical judgement were switched off at the source, and this is so even in those works where Lewis is most deeply and autobiographically engaged: "Cantleman shook noisily in the wicker chair like a dog or a fly-blown old gentleman" (*SH*, 111). This is *not* Lewis judging himself from the outside: rather an almost pathological depersonalization releases the personality itself from all favoritism, and prepares it to undergo a ceaseless mutability in its narrative qualifications. The same depersonalization can be observed at the level of the evaluation of character in the later, more "realistic" narratives, a level which is traditionally that on which the Implied Author's distance from and judgement of his characters can be measured. In many passages of such works, Lewis' official thematics assign unambiguous moral coordinates by which to "place" this or that choice or temptation of his characters: thus, when Pullman throws in his lot with the Bailiff, the very incarnation of the "Time and Youth Cults" denounced in *Time and Western Man*, it is at least externally clear that Pullman has fallen, and that he is to be read as the exemplar of corruption by the *Zeitgeist*. Yet such a judgement cannot function immanently: Lewis' narrative texture fails—yet the failure is surely deliberate —to provide anything like an ethical framework of the type of Jamesian irony: in James, to be sure, the reader (or Implied Author) is in a position to hold private or monadic experience together with an external moral perspective in the unity of a single act of consciousness.

Jamesian irony, therefore, unlike the judgements Lewis' narratives sometimes seem to project, unites point of view with ethical evaluation in an immanent way. From a historical point of view, however, the disintegration of the individual subject in Lewis is a later and more significant stage in the history of subjectivity than the uneasy equilibrium of Jamesian irony, and has the merit of marking a thoroughgoing problematization of the ethical itself.

It may be objected that the autonomy and incommensurability, in Lewis, of impersonal value and existential experience are very precisely the symptoms of some "dissociation of the moral sensibility" in Lewis himself. Yet as an ideological field, conceptions of ethics depend on a shared class or group homogeneity, and strike a suspicious compromise between the private experience of the individual and those values or functional needs of the collectivity which ethics rewrites or recodes in terms of interpersonal relationships. The social and political reality of the latter is thereby repressed and recontained by the archaic categories of good and evil, long since unmasked by Nietzsche as the sedimented traces of power relationships and the projections of a centered, quasi-feudal consciousness. In our time, ethics, wherever it makes its reappearance, may be taken as the sign of an intent to mystify, and in particular to replace the more complex and ambivalent judgements of a more properly political and dialectical perspective with the more comfortable simplifications of a binary myth. It will become abundantly clear that one part of Lewis' mind—the political and journalistic—is powerfully locked into the ideological closure of ethics and has become a virtual machine for issuing judgements and anathemata. The narratives, on the other hand, may be seen as the experimental or laboratory situation in which the very problem of making such judgements is itself foregrounded, and in which the impossibility of the ethical becomes itself the implicit center of the text, whose operations systematically and critically undermine this older "habit," this henceforth historically outmoded system of positioning the individual subject.

What remains of this last in Wyndham Lewis' narrative system may perhaps best be conveyed by a juxtaposition of the metamorphoses of the heroes of *The Childermass* with the superficially analogous moments in *Ulysses,* where the Nighttown section releases Mr. Bloom to an equally delirious and unpremeditated acting out of his most marginal daytime fantasies and private thoughts: "Under an arch of triumph Bloom appears bareheaded, in a crimson velvet mantle trimmed with ermine, bearing Saint Edward's staff. . . . Bloom with asses' ears seats himself in the pillory with crossed arms, his feet protruding. . . . A charming soubrette with dauby cheeks, mustard hair and large male hands and nose, leering mouth. . . . Pigeonbreasted, bottleshouldered, padded, in nondescript juvenile grey and black striped suit, too small for him, white tennis shoes, bordered stockings with turnover tops, and a red school cap with badge. . . ." etc. It would not be wrong, but too simple, to observe that, far from dissolving the personality into its external determinations, as Lewis' transformations do, the Joycean phantasmagoria serves to reconfirm the unity of the psyche, and to reinvent that depth-psychological perspective from which these various private fantasies spring. What is more significant in the present context is the way in which, in Joyce, the "visions" are organized with a view towards unity of tone and staged with a well-nigh sensory and hallucinatory intensity. The Nighttown scene in *Ulysses* is governed by that peculiar aesthetic structure which Freud called "the uncanny," and in which a represented event becomes intrinsically marked as the repetition of an older and archaic fantasy of which no independent traces remain in the text. This "return of the repressed" makes itself felt by the garish and technicolor representation of what is given as an essentially black-and-white reality, figures as daubed and rouged as in photorealist painting, objects de-realized by the very plenitude of their sensory being, by which the merely perceptual is unmasked as obsession. In Lewis, however, it is not the unification but rather the dispersal of subjectivity which is aimed at. Homogeneity of tone is neither desired nor achieved, and the successive transformations of the individual characters undermine the visual status of any individual metamorphosis and betray its origins in verbal cliché.

The status of the individual subject in Lewis cannot ultimately be described, let alone understood, unless we replace it in that peculiar narrative situation in which it is fixed and from which it depends: what we have hitherto termed the agon, the relational or dialogical axis of which "characters" become the merest poles. It is clear, for instance, not merely that the "relationship" between Bloom and Stephen has nothing structurally in common with the team of Pullman and Satters, but even more significantly that in Joyce each of the two major characters retains a monadic unity which has vanished from Lewis' tandem treatment of his couple.

Yet this is a very different relational category from the conventional pairing of lovers or partners, of siblings or rivals; we need a different word to convey the symbiotic "unity" of this new "collective" subject, both reduplicated and divided all at once. It is therefore useful to borrow Samuel Beckett's term for similar character relationships in his own work, and to designate as the *pseudo-couple*[11] all those peculiar and as yet imperfectly studied pairs in literary history which reach well beyond the twin "heroes" of *The Childermass* and the familiar Beckett teams of Vladimir and Estragon, Hamm and Clov, Mercier and Camier, through Flaubert's Bouvard and Pécuchet (and the less articulated pseudo-couple of Frédéric and Deslauriers in *L'Education sentimentale*) all the way back to Faust and Mephistopheles, and beyond them, to *Don Quixote*.

11. Samuel Beckett, "The Unnameable," in *Three Novels* (New York: Grove, 1965), p. 297.

The pseudo-couple is masculine; and Jean Borie's provocative thesis, that the nineteenth-century novel is essentially—even where the novelist himself is technically married—a *literature of bachelors*,[12] suggests that the male pseudo-couple might be understood as a kind of compensation formation, a curious structural halfway house in the history of the subject, between its construction in bourgeois individualism and its disintegration in late capitalism. The partners of the pseudo-couple are neither active, independent subjects in their own right, nor have they succumbed to the schizophrenic fetishization which characterizes contemporary consciousness. They remain legal subjects who nonetheless lack genuine autonomy and find themselves thereby obliged to lean on one another in a simulation of psychic unity which is little better than neurotic dependency.

In the present context, however, the pseudo-couple must first and foremost be understood as a structural device for preserving narrative as such. It is a commonplace of literary history that the extinction of the older passions, ambitions, and interests by *ennui* and *anorexia* necessarily generates the new formal permutation of the plotless novel with its "antihero," of which Flaubert's *Sentimental Education* once again marks the full-blown emergence. Nor has the experience of collective relations and group dynamics yet been historically strong enough to generate the new postindividualistic narrative forms by which such compromise formations could be superseded. In such a situation, the pseudo-couple provides the unique, unstable, acrobatic resolution of a structural *tour de force*. Now a stroll through an impersonal lnadscape can be recuperated from pure lyric or from the schizophrenic text by transforming it, as in *Bouvard et Pécuchet,* into a promenade in tandem. Now the empty stasis of Baudelairean *ennui* can be retrieved for narrative time by the copresence of the

12. Jean Borie, *Le Tyran timide* (Paris: Klincksieck, 1973), and *Le Célibataire français* (Paris: Le Sagittaire, 1976). See also Edward W. Said, *Beginnings* (New York: Basic Books, 1975), pp. 137–152.

pseudo-couple of *Waiting for Godot*. Meanwhile, a guard rail has been placed on that hallucinatory instability which, in *The Temptation of Saint Anthony*, threatens to engulf the subject altogether, and with it, the subject's narrative; the pseudo-couple complacently emerges from the sandstorms of unreality with its armature intact.

We are now in a better position to measure the function of the pseudo-couple as a molar reunification of molecular impulses that threaten dispersal; as the reimposition of a framework that allows powerfully antinarrative tendencies to be safely renarrativized, and the recontainment of an essentially centrifugal production of style. The pseudo-couple at once reveals and betrays the inner truth of what we have hitherto called the agon, of which it is the hypostasis, and which it retroactively unmasks as a pseudo-agon in its turn: a reification of struggle arrested and transmuted into static structural dependency.

The agon must thus be decisively distinguished from the powerful Hegelian dialectic of the Master and the Slave, which it at first seemed superficially to resemble. It is, indeed, to this moment of Hegel's *Phenomenology* as the structuralist concept of the binary opposition is to genuine dialectical contradiction: a mirror reduction of the latter which empties it of any genuinely negative force and flattens it into the static two-dimensionality of a graph or mathematical equation. The Hegelian struggle for recognition becomes in the pseudo-agon a mere vicious circle; while the third term of the Hegelian situation, that resistance of matter on which the slave must labor and from which History emerges, has here, as we have seen, been systematically effaced.

Now we may reread Nathalie Sarraute's account of the subconversation in a somewhat different way:

> These inner dramas composed of attacks, triumphs,
> recoils, defeats, caresses, bites, rapes, murders,
> generous renunciations or humble submissions, all
> have one thing in common: they cannot do without a

partner. . . . He is preeminently the catalyzer, the stimulant, thanks to whom these movements are set in motion, the obstacle that gives them cohesion, that keeps them from growing soft from ease and gratuitousness, or from going round and round in circles in the monotonous indigence of ruminating on one thing. He is the threat, the real danger as well as the prey that brings out their alertness and their suppleness, the mysterious element whose unforeseeable reactions, by making them continually start up again and evolve towards an unknown goal, accentuate their dramatic nature.[13]

Yet the "unknown goal" posited by Sarraute proves in our context to be mere repetition; while it is the cyclical closure of the pseudo-agon that generates all of the violent impulses so usefully enumerated in her text. Aggressivity in Lewis is therefore not some private characteristic of the novelist which diverts the narrative into the service of its own extrinsic gratifications: it is structurally inherent in the agon itself, in that utterly distinct from Hegelian or dialectical negativity, and expresses the rage and frustration of the fragmented subject at the chains that implacably bind it to its other and its mirror image.

13. Nathalie Sarraute, "Conversation and Sub-conversation," in *The Age of Suspicion*, translated by Maria Jolas (New York: Braziller, 1963), pp. 93–95.

3/
THE EPIC AS CLICHÉ, THE CLICHÉ AS EPIC

Sound and image sullenly mate; but the denser name
doubly impending bears down the simulacrum.
The Childermass

THE SUBCONVERSATION THUS AT ONCE
generates the closure of a rigid narrative
form in time; what we have not yet taken
into consideration is its vertical structure,
for it is evident that this vision of some
more authentic, yet unspoken, language
stirring beneath the banal language of a reified everyday
life necessarily presupposes what it wants to cancel, must
reinvent and textually reproduce the very surface it means
to undermine. There thus comes into being a surcharged
text, a palimpsest in which what is cancelled and *aufge-
hoben* must continue to be visible and readable behind the
cancellations that draw their value from it, as in a kind of
transgression.

Initially, no doubt, this stereoptic possibility is secured
by a relentless expansion and distortion of the primary
situation itself—now the raw material on which the "secondary" or subconversational text must work—a dilation

of daily life into the transparent immobility of the external afternoons, the eternal teas and Sunday morning strolls of Proustian narrative, its deceleration into that strange slow-motion sleepwalking tempo in which the audible reply hangs fire and echoes for long pages swarming with realer, tacit interactions, those of the "pregnant" or "meaning-ful" silences of Henry James, or of the breathless stillness of Faulknerian monologue, or yet again, that charged and menacing silence of Wyndham Lewis' characters, a silence of repressed violence "of such a quality that if it continued but a very little longer, spontaneous combustion must oc-cur in response to it" (*RL*, 235).

The differences between the various practitioners of the dialogical novel can be expected to emerge not only from the way which each conceives of that reified appear-ance to be subverted by the subconversation, but more tangibly, from the aesthetic or language practice designed to give the latter voice and verbal expression. At one ex-treme, the novelist can simply *explain* the deeper significance of the insignificant words and gestures of his characters, taking their banal and realistic, desultory con-versations apart as it were with tweezers, from above, painstakingly expounding the new pattern of clues con-cealed in an otherwise indifferent reality. The originality of Henry James was indeed to have projected this analytic capacity back into his characters themselves, who thus be-come virtual specialists in text grammar or speech act the-ory, their reflexions constituting a veritable *metalanguage* with respect to the conversational raw material on which they work ("the 'everything' clearly struck him, to the point even of determining his reply," "there were more-over the other facts of the selection and decision that this demonstration of her own had required," etc.).

At the other extreme, we find a novelist like Nathalie Sarraute herself attempting to characterize the quality of such interaction globally and as though from the outside, in the form of an image or *metaphor*, most frequently that

obsessive organic imagery which inspires the narrator of
Martereau to feel that other people "irresistibly secrete on
contact with me a substance like the liquid which certain
species give off to blind their prey."

The practice of Lewis is in this context exemplary in
allowing us to read the phenomenon of the surcharged text
as a commentary, not only on the increasing reification of
social life, but also on the exhaustion of form, on the way
in which the older realistic paradigms ceaselessly consume
their own primary material and render it obsolete. The
dialectic of innovation in the art of capitalism is best initially grasped, not in terms of formal invention, as the
apologists of modernism have generally described it, but in
terms of the exhaustion of the content of older forms,
which, given paradigmatic expression in the great realistic
novels, is thereby at once institutionalized, reappropriated
and alienated. The initial narrative expressions of such
situations as the love spat between Tarr and Bertha examined in the previous chapter is itself initially a critical and
negative act, the "realistic" correction of preexisting
stereotypes of such relationships, the narrative rectification
of the sentimental or aristocratic paradigms of previous
cultures. This analytical and demystifying symbolic act is
then itself reincorporated into what Marcuse calls "affirm-
ative" or legitimating, establishment culture, and its original sense disappears. So it is, for example, that today the
most vital contemporary "realisms"—and there are few
enough of them—draw their vitality from the marginality
of their content, from their historical good fortune in having as their raw material social realities which the dominant culture has not wished to see, let alone to express (as
in women's literature, black culture, or gay or colonial
literature).

A modernism such as that of Lewis must therefore
adopt a kind of second-degree or reflexive, reactive strategy, in which the blurred outlines of the older narrative
paradigm or proairetic unity remain in place, but are

violently restructured. The modernist renewal must be effectuated within the confines of dead storytelling conventions which remain massively in place, in a world already overinfected with culture and dead forms and with a stifling weight of dead ideas. In this situation the novelist is less a creative than a performing artist. His primary text, his "book" or script, is given him from the outset, in the form of the banal situations and stereotypes of a degraded everyday life, gossipy women, impecunious Bohemia, a dreary sentimental entanglement; while his "composition" of these scenes proves in reality to be an *interpretation* of them in much the same way that an actor's voice restores vitality to a faded text. So at this late hour in Western culture the novelist must intervene in his very situations themselves, speaking on behalf of the gestures of his characters, which are henceforth too commonplace to discharge any intrinsic meaning of their own.

For the mediocre lovers' quarrel, for Tarr's clumsy gesture of affection which solves nothing, must be substituted an alternative and reorganized story-line, some bustling and lively second-degree narrative which rises on the rubble and the fragments of the first "realistic" one:

> Docilely she covered him with her inertia. He was supposed to be performing a miracle of bringing the dead to life. Gone about too crudely, the willing mountebank, Death, had been offended: it is not thus that great spirits are prevailed upon to flee. Her 'indifference'—the great, simulated and traditional —would not be ousted by an upstart and younger relative. By Tarr himself, grown repentant, yes. But not by another 'indifference'. (*T*, 50)

As with all the most concentrated specimens of modern writing, the principal difficulty of such a passage lies neither in its content nor in the complexity of its figures, but rather in the demand it makes upon us to invent a wholly new way of reading, ad hoc, for the exclusive purposes of this particular style or "private language." The situation is one which would be conveyed by the movie camera in a single frame; the woman dutifully embracing an equally unenthusiastic man. But the reader has a series of complicated operations to perform before this expressive still materializes. Indeed, the figural level proves to be a complex allegorical narrative, which must itself be reconstructed from fragmentary data before the first "literal" scene can be reconstructed and substituted for it in its turn. The estrangement of the simple visual datum of the tepid embrace into mouth-to-mouth resuscitation generates a quasi-Elizabethan allegory in which the personified figure of Death refuses to be conjured by half-hearted means. The reader is thus required to invest more energy in the preliminary reinvention or recreation, the inner visual staging, of this elaborate vehicle than in the decipherment of any realistic representation; and this well before any question as to its tenor can hope to be raised. Once reconstructed, it is the allegorical narrative as a whole which then allows us to guess the literal tableau which was the object of the reading in the first place.

This complex narrative operation thus involves a four-term process. The novelist establishes an initial "literal" (which is to say, "fictive") situation, only immediately to fragment it into the building blocks and components of a new allegorical and textual narrative which has little enough thematic relationship to the original. The reader is then obliged to begin with the fragments of the allegory, which must be reconstructed in narrative form before the first-degree or "realistic" narrative can be deduced and inserted beneath the text as the latter's "signified."

Yet this signified exists nowhere: it is an evanescent effect of the reader's own "prior knowledge" or existential experience, which comes before him/her with the force of something already known, something recognized, rather than witnessed for the first time. Such a passage thereby dramatizes the dialectic of the private language in modernism at the same time that it betrays the dilemma to which the latter constitutes a willful and desperate, impossible solution: the disintegration of the literary exchange, as a socially guaranteed and institutionalized compact between writer and reader; the disappearance of a shared code, and the problematization of even those proairetic linguistic unities or naming systems which allow us to feel that we are discussing the same shared universe; the *anomie* and fragmentation of social life itself, which systematically dissolves the older classes and the homogeneous publics that developed out of them, at the same time that it isolates the now equivalent monads of the market system so effectively from one another that the writing monad can entertain no realistic hope of awakening analogous private experience or personal reference in the equally monadic reader.

Lewis' narrative practice, in the passage we have just quoted, makes it plain that this dilemma can be bracketed by a modernism consequent enough to jettison the mirage-ideal of intersubjective communication altogether. The text does not reproduce the process, or the data, of Lewis' own inner vision and demand that we raise ourselves to its imaginative level: rather it merely proposes a certain number of mental operations, of which the final step is the breath of life, the infusion of private experience or personal knowledge which can have no possible correspondence or relationship of adequation with Lewis' own, always assuming that he had such an original vision, or experience, or imaginative starting point, to begin with. The reader's reconstruction of that "starting point" is quite properly unverifiable and undecidable and serves merely as a sign that the operations have been performed and the reading completed, rather than as any approximation to Lewis' "original intent." Yet the absence of this authorial referent is itself masked in turn by the immense energies released by our own demanding practice as readers: whence the exhiliration that unexpectedly takes the place of the more predictable pathos that such an experience of the breakdown of social language ought logically to inspire.

No little part of such energies and such exhilaration springs from the persistence of narrative in this passage, and from our obligation to reconstruct its data, twice over, in narrative form. Paradoxically, the thoroughgoing subversion of the raw materials and narrative categories of traditional or even realistic storytelling does not annihilate the latter so much as it causes it to be reinvented afresh, as it were *ab ovo,* in a return to the most primitive anecdotal techniques. Yet the implicit reinvention of narrative in modern literature must necessarily lack all the stark monumentality, all the grim gestural simplicity, of the emergent storytelling forms of the time of Dante and Giotto, of Boccaccio: for it is no longer with the freshness of origins in a void and in an untouched language that literature itself can here reemerge. The pastiche of Elizabethan language is the more relevant one, evoking a situation in which dusty plots and stereotypical paradigms are freshened and revived, not in some new first-degree representational narrative, but rather within that second-degree speech which is the theatrical language of the characters of the now dramatized original paradigm and which thus stands, less as its mimesis, than as its implicit and explicit commentary.

In much the same way, the novelist "edits" his footage and like a movie-maker transforms the data of his initial narrative material into a finished montage, into a purely cinematographic language or sign system that obeys quite different laws from those of the original prose "idea." In so doing, he would appear to have reversed the priorities of Coleridge's distinction between fancy and imagination: for what is operative in the texts here under consideration is the essentially decorative work of Fancy itself as it transforms the pregiven data of its original scenario into a host of textually interlinking subevents, swarming with molecular agitation. As for Imagination, the primal shaping power of the mind, the very source of plot formation in its most august Aristotelian sense, it has lived; and its dead monuments are what oppress creative spontaneity, its forms appropriated and trivialized by commodity culture.

Yet the older dead paradigms of the imagination do not for all that disappear: for it is against and upon them that fancy must articulate its productive activity, in a structure not without some similarity to what Martinet termed the "double articulation" of language itself, where "the units on the 'lower' level of phonology (the sounds of a language) have no function other than that of combining with one another to form the 'higher' units of grammar (words)."[1] For the writer, this lower level of exhausted words, exhausted stories, exhausted raw material, remains little more than a pretext; if anything, indeed, it is perhaps rather to the reader that something of the older function of imagination still falls. For it is the reader who is ultimately called upon to reinvent the external form itself, to mint the vast, slow curve of which the sentences are broken traces and fragments, to restore to the vivid microlife of the novelist's language that absent whole of which its moments are the parts.

This is not to say that the reader's work is done when the larger narrative unities have thereby been reconstructed. On the contrary, the same process awaits him/her within the individual sentences themselves, as the phenomenon of apposition in *The Childermass* will demonstrate under more microscopic analysis. The cataphoric epithet, indeed, enforces a preliminary passage through figure or allegory which reverses the "normal" order of the reading-reconstruction of the sentence no less unavoidably than does the expressionistic projection of the narrative situation. The syntactical rhythm of apposition, dangling before the fact, and drawn up tight by the sentence that

1. John Lyons, *Introduction to Theoretical Linguistics* (Cambridge: Cambridge University Press, 1969), p. 54. And see, for a relatively ahistorical application of this concept to aesthetic form, Claude Lévi-Strauss, *The Raw and the Cooked*, translated by John and Doreen Weightman (New York: Harper, 1970), pp. 18–30.

reels it in, signals the changing of slides on the machine, emits the click with which a new image, full-blown, emerges onto the screen of perception:

> A hieratic huge-headed bat, with raised arms the
> Bailiff protests in a thick patter of expostulation.
>
> (*CM*, 193)

Winglike draperies flapping on the waving arms, head poised as though for flight: the whole image is flattened like a silhouette against the backdrop of space, with nothing of the piecemeal life in time of normal perception, in which random scraps and clues are gradually unified into manageable perspectives. The image in Lewis thus reverses that impressionistic procedure which Proust characterized as a fidelity to perceptual experience itself, a presentation "of things in the order of our perceptions, rather than by first accounting for them by their causes."[2] Here, on the contrary, the Gestalt comes first: it is the nameable phenomenon in its totality which then governs the successive emergence of its various parts and components.

This order holds for the most complicated representations as well as those of simple gestures, so that it is the global characterization of the event which dictates its unfolding in time, as well as the latest transformations of its actors:

> The ox is felled: Satters as Keystone giant receives
> the crack exactly in the right spot, he sags forward
> in obedient overthrow, true to type—as though after
> a hundred rehearsals, true to a second—and crashes
> to earth as expected, rolling up a glazed eyeball
> galore, the correct Keystone corpse of Jack-the-
> Giantkiller comedy. (*CM*, 116)

The figural use of preexisting conventionalized roles (Keystone cops, Jack the Giantkiller) is itself inscribed in

---

2. Marcel Proust, *A la recherche du temps perdu* (Paris: Gallimard, Bibliothèque de la Pléiade, 1954, three volumes), I, 653.

the sentences as a slavish and comic "obedience" of reality to its own archetypes; the atomic elements of perception then racing to fill their appropriate stations in the Gestalt. Such a sentence is autoreferential in the way in which its ostensible content ("exactly in the right spot," "obedient," "true to type," "after a hundred rehearsals," "as expected," "correct") designates its own structure: the assimilation of the unknown, the temporally new, to the already known, the stereotype, the endlessly prerehearsed.

"It is a style," Kenner tells us, "composed of phrases, not actions"[3]: to which we have already added the proviso that the phrases, with their heterogeneous sources and references, are never completely subdued and mastered by the sentence as a larger unity. But this observation about the coexistence of ready-made, free-floating bits of speech can readily be converted into a statement about the figural content of such passages, which derives, not from symbolic structures inherent in the fable itself, but rather from some extrinsic and impersonal storehouse of cultural materials:

> Tying their chokers, trotting clowns hurrying at the crack of the magisterial circus-whip, the six scuttle and trip, but never fall, the ground rising in pustules at their feet to mock them, the wind clipping them on the ear, or pushing them upon the obstructions arranged for them to amuse the idiot-universe. They skip and dance on the bulky treacherous surface of the earth, stoic beneath nature's elemental hot-fisted cuffs, tumblers or Shakespearean clowns, punchballs got up as Pierrot. (*CM*, 132–133)

The shifting appositions (circus clowns, Shakespearean clowns, Pierrots) program the events of the sentence in progress, and, themselves received images, are reflected in the outer form of the language itself as a constant reshuffling of received idiom ("hot-fisted cuffs" as a

---

3. Hugh Kenner, *Wyndham Lewis* (Norfolk, Ct.: New Directions, 1954), p. 15.

portmanteau of the expression "hot-tempered" and the word "fisticuffs," the whole then refashioned on the model of "tight-fisted").

The great sentences of Lewis have therefore little enough in common with that Flaubertian aesthetic of the "mot juste," of which Joyce, with his "artfully" placed adverbs and his traces of Paterian unction, is the hegemonic modernist realization. They give little enough aid and comfort to the modernist conviction that sense perception can ultimately be fully rendered in a sentence structure, that a "parole pleine" is possible, that the world really does exist to end up in a Book which will replace it and in which the glint of sunlight on a pond, the stir of wind upon the earth's surfaces, will thus forever gleam and mildly tremble in the eternal immobility of the printed sentence.

At the same time, there can be no doubt that Lewis fulfills another, and apparently quite different, tendency at work in the stylistic practice of Flaubert: that of the "sottisier" and the "dictionary of received ideas," the inventory of "bêtise," and the relish in the mindless use of stereotypes. How could it be otherwise, when the very mechanisms of Lewis' style presuppose our indispensable preliminary familiarity with the stereotypical epithets and appositions that inaugurate it and program its perceptions?

> Satters fully dressed is propped within, his lush bulk
> pitched against the jamb, occupying the breach in
> beefy sinuosity, his curled head bent somewhat to
> clear the lintel, his eyes cast archly up. The smile of
> Leonardo's St. John, appropriated to the features of a
> germanic ploughboy, sustains an expression of heavy
> mischief. (*CM*, 121)

Where the Joycean reading play opens a place for the spectator to witness Mr. Bloom's homosexual tendencies in all their rouged *coquetterie*, dissolving the cultural or advertising stereotypes into the merest pretexts for the simulacrum of a stage or music hall perception, in Lewis they preserve their autonomy; and the prestige of the no longer adequately visualizable masterpiece of Leonardo, diffused through Sunday rotogravures and banalized by art appreciation, shoots forth a distant and degraded ray to strike this passage with a spurious glow as the sign that this new face of Satters has been certified as "perceptible" by experts in some absent precinct of an official culture.

The collage-composition practiced by Lewis thus draws heavily and centrally on the warehouse of cultural and mass cultural cliché, on the junk materials of industrial capitalism, with its degraded commodity art, its mechanical reproduceability, its serial alienation of language, in short, with what the structuralists would call the Symbolic Order: that systematized network of cultural code and representation which preexists, speaks, and produces the individual subject by means of the ruse of a belief in individuality itself. In such a situation, the personal language, the private thought are themselves illusions, where conventionalized formulae dictate in advance the thought that had seemed to choose them for its own instruments. Nor can genuine experience be readily identified any longer, when a degraded culture intervenes between us and our objects, to substitute for them, by an imperceptible sleight of hand, some standardized snapshot. Whoever under such circumstances continues to believe in the unproblematical functioning of natural language falls most surely victim to this illusionistic structure which silently undoes its most "authentic" utterances.

This is the dilemma to which Lewis' linguistic praxis speaks in exemplary and ingenious fashion: his "method," if we can call it that, is to use the cliché against itself—or better still, to pit clichés on the level of gestural images against the verbal clichés with which the sentences themselves are hopelessly corroded. In this way, a kind of perceptual freshness is reinvented out of the unexpectedly virulent interaction of stale and faded substances. Witness the following account of Pullman's movements as he offers to help Satters to his feet:

> Stalking and stretching tense-legged, in a succession
> of classical art-poses suggestive of shadow-archery,
> he approaches Satters. He relaxes like the collapse of
> a little house of cards, extends a friendly lackadaisical
> hand, and sings out: 'Up again, come jump to it!'
>
> (*CM*, 19)

The visual cliché has here been broken into its component parts, then reverbalized into segments of linguistic commonplace such that the latter are unable to discharge their automatic meaning-effects, but, neutralized by discontinuity and each other's indifference, remain as empty imperatives to visualize the central gesture. Yet we must already know in advance what that gesture is, since the words have long since lost their capacity to convey new information:

> Pullman several times is parted from one of his slip-
> pers, having to stop to reinsert his foot and prise it
> up with humped toes. (*CM*, 27)

Without personal knowledge of the muscular operation that lends this sentence the force of a recall, it must deteriorate into a series of inert notations, as empty as an untranslatable hieroglyph.

> He sat upon a cushion, leoninely slumped back
> against the panelling, as if luxuriating in a technical
> knockout.   (*RL*, 156)

Such a sentence hangs uncertainly between two received images, the late-night glimpse of a besotted party-goer, and the newsreel snapshot of the boxer seated against the ropes: only the metaphorical term fails to intensify the literal one, but rather bears it off along with it into sheerest conventionality. What unexpectedly remains behind is however the unspecified place of their twin referent, the "real" Victor sprawling upon a material sofa in some unique moment of historical time—a vivid "idea" which the reader hastens to substitute for the tangible words that have ceased to function.

So it is that over the great moments in Lewis there hangs a strange and nagging sense of *déjà vu*. The very appearance of the Bailiff, for instance, strikes you as graphically as a cartoon character, or a creature out of fairy tales, as archetypal as all great character creation, yet as familiar as the household bogeyman:

> Tapping on the flags of the court with a heavy stick, his neck works in and out as though from a socket, with the darting reptilian rhythm of a chicken. His profile is balanced, as he advances, behind and before by a hump and a paunch. He wears a long and sombre caftan. His wide sandalled feet splay outwards as he walks at the angle and in the manner of a frog. No neck is visible, the chin appearing to issue from and return into the swelling gallinaceous chest. . . . He is all grinning vulpine teeth, puckered eyes, formidable declination of the ant-eating nose, rubicond cheeks, eyes of phosphor. The goatee waggles on the glazed bulbous chin; it is the diabolics of the most ancient mask in the world exulting in its appropriate setting. (*CM*, 130, 151)

We seem to *remember* such a figure, which surely did not need to wait for Lewis to invent it. Yet Falstaff and Quasimodo are genuinely mythopoetic creations, whose elaboration is systematically fed and unified by their inner concepts (the latter fed in its turn by their transformation into cultural objects). Lewis' Bailiff is vivid, however, because he is put together out of the most heterogeneous bits and pieces each of which adds its own glint of borrowed intensity: the chickenwalk, the hump, the caftan, the devil's mask, all are pieced together as in a collage, and Lewis' "description" of the Bailiff is thus as dishonest and as artificial as the original himself.

Lewis' style would thereby seem to have voluntarily renounced the twin vocation of the greatest modern writing: to forge a new language, and with it to convey some hitherto unexperienced of an unfamiliar external world, as new as on the first day. Yet the loss is in reality a displacement; and Lewis' language, perversely misdirected by comparison with the traditional praxis of fictional discourse, proves to have unexpected affinities with the discursive formation of quite different narrative genres altogether.

"Milton in the language of Swift": the force of Hugh Kenner's characterization of *The Human Age* no doubt springs from the unforeseen reversal in which it is the poet rather than the prose fabulist who now comes before us as the maker of plots and the quintessential storyteller. And there can be no doubt that we return to *Paradise Lost* with new eyes when, after a reading of *The Human Age*, we grasp the older epic as an exemplum of theological science fiction.

Yet the affinities run deeper than this: for artificial epic, from Vergil to that last and ripest of the Romantic narratives, the *Pan Tadeusz* of Mickiewicz, is an eclectic structure which combines poetic and narrative modes in a determinate and "impure" fashion that allows neither to be fully realized in its own terms. Unlike genuine epic, with its formulaic basis and its preliterate context, artificial epic emerges into a world in which prose narrative already exists, and to which it therefore stands in the generic relationship of a formal alternative, both reaction and negation all at once. Unlike prose narrative, artificial epic takes as its object of representation not events and actions themselves but rather the describing of them: the process whereby such narrative raw materials are fixed and immobilized in the heightened and embellished speech of verse. There is thus already present in epic discourse a basic and constitutive rift between form and content, between the words and their objects—a rift which prose narrative and lyric seek in their varying fashions to abolish, but upon maintaining which the vitality of artificial epic depends.

The heroic simile is one of the principal agents of this separation, and functions as a *sign* that a degraded and contingent reality (the dreary anxiety of warfare, the privations of long journeys, persistent hard luck and the cheapness of human life) has achieved transmutation into monumental flourish or arabesque, that from the chaos of ordinary experience the eternal geometry of epic decoration has been triumphantly disengaged:

> Poi si rivolse, e parve di coloro
> che corrono a Verona il drappo verde
> per la campagna; e parve di costoro
> quelli che vince, non colui che perde.[4]

Yet from the purely visual standpoint, we perceive little enough, neither seeing Messire Bruno as he hurries to rejoin his companions, nor witnessing the race at Verona. Rather, the first act is merely narrated for us by Dante, while the second one we *remember*. The topical allusion jogs a storehouse within the mind of what must not too hastily be assimilated to Platonic ideas or Jungian archetypes: some fund of memory-traces in which there persevere images of quintessential forms and movements, idealized gestures, that "formidable erosion of contours" of which Gide, following Nietzsche, liked to speak, a kind of stark simplification of the empirical. From such a source there rises, not the stricken face and trembling ribcage of some flesh-and-blood Olympic runner in a newsreel, but rather the eternal runner himself, shoulders flung back, billowed about by draperies, slowly letting off as the ribbon flutters slackly to the ground around his feet. This is the sense in which Mnemosyne presides over the epic, for the epic does not, like the novel, give us to see as though for the first time, but rather depends and draws on, lives by the restimulation of, this older preexisting gestural repertoire.

---

4. *Inferno*, Canto XV, lines 121–124. Binyon translates as follows:

> He turned, and seemed like, in the field before
> Verona, one of those who ran the race
> For the green cloth; so seemed he running, nor
> Seemed in the loser's but the winner's place.

(*The Portable Dante*, ed. Paolo Milano [New York: Viking, 1949], p. 83).

It can therefore be asserted that the poet of artificial epic does not compose immediately with words, but rather works, as with his most fundamental raw materials and building blocks, with just such perceptual or gestural signifiers, juxtaposing and reunifying them into the sensuous continuity of the verse paragraph. The narrative, indeed, may be considered an organizational pretext for the alignment and quasi-spatial projection of just such perceptual unities as bodies in flight or ships at sea:

> *Satan* with less toil, and now with ease
> Wafts on the calmer wave by dubious light,
> And like a weather-beaten Vessel holds
> Gladly the Port, though Shrouds and Tackle torn;
> Or in the emptier waste, resembling Air,
> Weighs his spread wings . . .

games in the Elysian Fields:

> Largior hic campos aether et lumine vestit
> purpureo, solemque suum, sua sidera norunt.
> Pars in gramineis exercent membra palaestris,
> contendunt ludo, et fulva luctantur harena;
> pars pedibus plaudunt choreas et carmina dicunt.

the slow rotation of the heavenly bodies, but also the gesture of the sower:

> et Ruth se demandait,
> Immobile, ouvrant l'oeil à moitié sous ses voiles,
> Quel dieu, quel moissonneur de l'éternel été,
> Avait, en s'en allant, négligemment jeté
> Cette faucille d'or dans le champ des étoiles.

The external form of the language (whether strophic composition, terza rima, or the hexameter itself) then seals and reduplicates this inner composition by gestural or perceptual unities. Its metric units thus stand as the outer emblems and the material substitutes of the inner forms, and tangibly signal the substitution, for the flux of daily life, of these new *essences*. The verse of the epic is thus the linguistic mimesis, not of the original empirical data, but rather of precisely this molar reunification and gestural incorporation of the disparate and the contingent.

It is no accident that, just as the epic Flaubert of *Salammbô* coexists with the Flaubert of the *sottisier*, so also in Lewis, alongside what we have called the "satire-collage," there unexpectedly emerge ruined sheets of just such epic decoration:

> Two birds, one immediately above the other, appear to be approaching the heavenly city. As however their bodies get sufficiently near, they are seen to be not two birds but one. What seemed like two is a large bird of unusual size holding something in its beak. Crossing the highroad at the further extremity of the camp, it describes a wide arc that takes it southward and to the rear of the Bailiff's court. Thence, flying with unhesitating precision, it sweeps towards the watching crowd. Skimming the summit of the official box, neck outstretched, its face seems, as it rushes overhead, like that of an ecstatic runner. It flies directly to a basalt slab situated between the Bailiff's enclosure and the ferry station. As it touches the heavenly soil a roar of faint trumpets comes from the city. At the same time a mirage rises from the further edge of the water, having the consistency and tint of a wall of cheese, but cut into terraces full of drowsy movement which are reflected in the stream.
>
> (*CM*, 140)

The fading of the epic voice, the gradual ebbing of the high style to the point where it can accommodate the peculiar magnification of the friable layers of a cross-section of cheese, is quite different from the exhilarating shifts in Joycean registers ("And they beheld Him even Him, ben Bloom Elijah, amid clouds of angels ascend to the glory of the brightness at an angle of forty-five degrees over Donohoe's in Little Green Street like a shot off a shovel"). The withdrawal of Lewis' language from his vision rather opens a space in which the chaotic glint of epic lances and the humble vegetables of still life or genre painting for a fitful instant coexist. It would seem, indeed, that such aesthetics as those of Flaubert and Lewis, which so inexplicably provide for a shifting of gears between the epic and the satiric modes, imply some more fundamental kinship between their respective raw materials. Both kinds of content can in fact be subsumed under Barthes' notion of the proairetic code; yet this peculiar coexistence of cliché and gestured archetype suggests that the concept of the pro-airetic code itself demands to be radically historicized.

The truth is that what we have called gestural archetypes are in reality nothing but clichés also: only they are clichés *before the fall,* the received ideas of an older and socially more vital culture, of the preindustrial city-state, with its festivals and armies, its personalized quasi-feudal power relationships, its sophisticated pageants and processions, and at the same time, its proximity to the life of the fields that surround it (in this sense, the life of the Bailiff's camp is at least colonial, if not really preindustrial). In the *polis*, which has overcome what Marx and Engels called the "rural idiocy" of the neolithic village, without yet having been developed out of all proportion to individual life by the dynamics of capitalism, cliché and received idea are no more than the form taken by collective intelligence itself: they are the shared experience, gathered into images, of the *Gemeinschaft*.

So it is that the essential difference between artificial epic and satire-collage, between the high style of *Salammbô* or of the above passage, and the low style of *Tarr* or *Bouvard et Pécuchet,* is not a generic or stylistic one, but rather the difference between two situations, a contextual variation between two distinct modes of production and two different moments of history. The satire-collage is the form taken by artificial epic in the degraded world of commodity production and of the mass media: it is artificial epic whose raw materials have become spurious and inauthentic, monumental gesture now replaced by the cultural junk of industrial capitalism. This is why the most authentic realization of the ancient epic ideal in modern times yields not some decorative and beautified pastiche, but rather the most jarring and energetic mimesis of the mechanical, and breathes a passionate revulsion for that great automobile graveyard which is the "modern mind."

4/
THE PICTURE-HOUSE
OF THE SENSES

But the terrible perquisite of the blind was there in the
staring, milky eyeballs: and an expression of ascetic
ponderous importance weighted it so that, mean as it
was, in reality, this mask was highly impressive. Also,
from its bitter immunity and unquestioned right-of-way,
and from the habit of wandering through the outer
jungle of physical objects, it had the look that some
small boy's face might acquire, prone to imagine himself
a steamroller, or a sightless Juggernaut.

The Wild Body

 HERE REMAINS THE PROBLEM OF THE
ultimate meaning of such stylistic prac-
tice, of the intent and passion that moti-
vates so many false sentences, tirelessly
combining amalgams of words whose
function is no longer to reproduce the
real, but quite the contrary, to testify to our powerlessness
to do so and to the inescapable contamination of the collective mind and of language itself. In modern times, however, all creative and original speech flows from privation
rather than from plenitude: its redoubled energies, far
from tapping archaic or undiscovered sources of energy,
are proportionate to the massive and well-nigh impenetrable obstacles which aesthetic production must overcome
in the age of reification.

In such a situation, the prodigious force with which
Wyndham Lewis propagates his bristling mechanical sentences and hammers the reified world into a forbiddingly
cubist surface may be thought of as a virtual cooptation of

the machine, a homeopathic expropriation of its alienated dynamism. In Lewis, indeed, the machine seems to have absorbed all the vitality of the human beings henceforth dependent on it:

> After a brief disturbance within, there came a mighty purr from its recesses, then an outsize and very handsome dove-grey roadster emerged. Its blunt imposing head appeared unexpectedly quickly for such an important accouchement, riding with drowsy power over the obstructions of the uneven soil. Victor was at the wheel. This monster, as it moved across the yard, was gathering speed; it melted ponderously through the ungated entrance at the side of the hotel, bellowing like a pole-axed bullock. A hand waved to it, unnoticed, from an upper window, the words 'Good Luck!' accompanied the flutter of the flesh, with salutation and godspeed. Next moment it had sunk away, with velvet self-effacement, rolling upon a carpet of rich dust, which changed into a low-lying fog upon the road, sucked in at the gateway for some time after the great car had departed.   (*RL,* 300)

Such an apparition, at the very climax of *The Revenge for Love,* stands as the virtual personification of what Sartre has called the *practico-inert,* that malignant destiny or antifreedom which human beings create over against themselves by the investment and alienation of their labor in objects which return upon them unrecognizably, in the hostile form of a mechanical Necessity.[1] The motorcar is indeed the very locus of metonymic fission, which, transmitted to ever wider circles of objects, ends by drawing life itself (the slaughtered bullock, the "flutter of flesh") into its baleful dominion.

It is thus less a thing than a center of radiant energy; and seems to bear Victor and Margot forward of its own will upon their fatal journey. For Margot, indeed, the machine is an uncontrollable destiny which nonetheless, per-

---

1. Jean-Paul Sartre, *Critique of Dialectical Reason* (London: New Left Books, 1976), translated by Alan Sheridan-Smith, pp. 161–196.

versely and unaccountably, requires our own collusion and accuses our complicity:

> To devour miles and eat up minutes, in gulp after gulp, use must be made of *her* organs, so it seemed, as well as its own. Under her feet she had a time-eating and space-guzzling automaton, rather than a hackneyed means of transport, however horridly high-powered. It was *her* time, too, it was gobbling up—under great pressure, in big passionate draughts. (*RL*, 317)

So paradoxically the monadic isolation of the subject has been overcome: but as though through some grisly misunderstanding, through some blind alienation from without, which cannot be observed but merely felt, like the wrenching away, in wind and flood, of some windowless dwelling.

Yet this painful dislocation of consciousness, battered from without by the meteoric storm of history, now at last provides material for narrative and can be expressed. The expression remains a private matter: for the monad still only contemplates the shadows on its own wall of some *Ding-an-sich* it will never be in a position to confront directly. Yet the approach of the Real is unmistakable, if only as the absent cause of what are very real subjective effects:

> Meanwhile trees, rocks, and telegraph poles stood up dizzily before her and crashed down behind. They were held up stiffly in front of her astonished eyes, then snatched savagely out of the picture. Like a card-world, clacked cinematographically through its static permutations by the ill-bred fingers of a powerful conjurer, everything stood upon end and then fell flat. He showed you a tree—a cardboard tree. Fix your eye upon this! he said. Then with a crash it vanished. Similarly with a segment of cliff. Similarly with a telegraph-pole. Her head ached with the crash of images. Every time a telegraph-pole fell down she felt the shock of its collapse in the picture-house of the senses. (*RL*, 316)

The instinctive greatness of Lewis was, I think, to have understood that even where the real is ultimately inaccessible we are not for all that reduced to silence. The impressionistic way kept faith with the illusions of subjectivity and sought lovingly to reproduce them in the detail of their appearance. Lewis' expressionism on the contrary marks those illusions with the stamp of their own spuriousness, keeping the place of the Real warm by deforming its caricatural substitutes in the realm of the sheerly phenomenal.

So it is that Margot comes face to face with the most indigestible fact of external reality itself, with that outermost fact, which, spelling the dissolution of the monad itself, can never be interiorized: in short, with death itself, in the person of the guardia civil head-on in their path. The dead guard, who for the lovers unites the guilt of murder with the certainty of their own death sentence, thus signals a reality too scandalous to penetrate the mind, a reality that blows upon us in fitful, intermittent snatches, like a word on the tip of the tongue, or the memory of an illumination we cannot quite recapture. This is how Margot receives her ultimate glimpse of what defeats human life, of that by which love is itself annihilated:

> Far worse than that, she discovered herself at last watching against her will the floodlit stretch of rust-red road. Plumes of dust were spurting up; but their car (it had left her behind) was rapidly disappearing and had already grown quite small, in diminishing perspective; while in the foreground she was staring down at a disagreeable flattened object. Sprawling in the centre of the road, it was incredibly two-dimensional and, in short, unreal. It might have just been painted upon the earth. But it looked more like a big untidy pattern, cut out of black paper, except for what was the face. That was flat, as well—as flat as a pancake, but as pale as a sheet, with a blue smear where the chin was. It was the chin of Prussian-blue. The flat black headgear of a Civil Guard, likewise no thicker than cardboard, lay a foot away from the head. (*RL*, 329)

So the trick is turned, and the impossible, unimaginable picture nonetheless imagined in all its impossibility! This astonishing passage is of course not meant to represent Margot's perception of the corpse (in reality, she is herself swiftly disappearing inside the car she imagines to be diminishing in the distance) but reproduces her attempt to visualize it in its absence as the transfer of inadequate and incompatible images onto the wall of her mind. In some regressive and prelogical backroom of consciousness, indeed, our spontaneous first thought is likely to be that a man run over by a car is flat as a pancake, and pale as a sheet. Unlike Margot, however, on her infantile level, and unlike Lewis, on his reflexive one, we ourselves repress the unlikely first thought in the name of the reality principle of common sense and scientific rationality. Yet we thereby emerge from our first naïve vision empty-handed, into an imaginative void in which we no longer quite know what we are allowed to say about this lifeless body: bloodied, bruised, broken in places like a doll—all of these are a whistling in the dark, conveying not vision, but the attempt to stimulate it artificially and to inspire some adequate representation, some "correct" reflexion of reality, which is not forthcoming.

Lewis', however, is not a child-art; unlike, say, a Faulkner, he is uninterested in the attempt to do justice to the existential limits of the child's prerational consciousness. The passage in question is in fact part of a thoroughgoing critique of Margot's immaturity, and of the cultural forces which have left her thus defenseless. The child-vision is here, as it were in Hegelian fashion, cancelled and assimilated to a higher form of critical consciousness, in which it is however preserved, in the instant of being denied on its own terms. It is as though this language overcomes some initial muteness before the incommensurability of experience (Mallarmé's sterility, the silences of modern literature and modern music, of modern philosophy) by concluding, in a "bustling" and energetic gesture, that since it cannot tell us what to see, it will rather tell us what we would have seen had it been able to do so. Since there exists no adequate language for "rendering" the object, all that is left to the writer is to tell us how he would have rendered it had he had such a language in the first place.

There thus comes into being a language beyond language, shot through with the jerry-built shoddiness of modern industrial civilization, brittle and impermanent, yet full of a mechanic's enthusiasm. Lewis' style is thus a violent and exemplary figure for the birth of all living speech and turns to its own advantage the discovery that all language is a second-best, the merest substitute for the impossible plenitude of a primary language that has never existed. In this sense all speech must settle its accounts with the optical illusion of a natural language if it is to be delivered from a terrorized reduction to silence. So Lewis' style, the only true English futurism, an immense hangar in which we may still learn to tap the almost extinct sources of language production, does not in the clattering, deafening noise of its own mechanical processes seek to be preserved as an icon in its own right, but rather consents to its own abolition in time, freeing us in turn from the fetishistic spell of style itself.

5/
FROM NATIONAL ALLEGORY
TO LIBIDINAL APPARATUS

The history of our century would not be one mainly of
personalities. . . . What we should see would be big,
ideologic currents, gaudily coloured, converging,
dissolving, combining or contending. It would look like
a chart of the ocean rather than a Madame Tussaud's
Waxworks; though there would be faces (one with a
tooth-brush moustache), like labels of one or other of
the big currents of ideas. . . . So there would be
arabesques of creation and destruction, the personal
factor unimportant, the incarnations of ideas, the
gigantic coloured effigies of a Hitler or a Stalin, no more
than the remains of a monster advertisement.

Self Condemned

EWIS, UNREAD, IS CUSTOMARILY LUMPED
together for convenience with the great
modernists who were his sometime friends
or collaborators—Pound, Eliot, Joyce,
and Yeats—the latter having come to
form an exclusive and overisolated pantheon in that unexamined schema which passes the most
often for our notion of literary history. Yet this honor by
association does Lewis little good, I think, and only serves
to obscure the real nature of his originality.

Unlike the aforementioned writers, he was essentially a
political novelist. In this role he modelled himself by design as well as by temperament on the most dazzling and
successful craftsman in political art whom modern Britain
has known—namely, George Bernard Shaw.[1] Lewis

1. "I am just as genial a character as Mr. Bernard Shaw, to give you an idea.
I am rather what Mr. Shaw would have been like if he had been an artist—I here
use 'artist' in the widest possible sense—if he had not been an Irishman, if he

87

wished indeed to become an anti-Shaw, artistic technician (replacing music with painting) and journalist-ideologue all at once, this time using Nietzsche *against* the idea of progress; peopling his works with secondary characters who are his own spokesmen, though the socialist chauffeurs and mechanics of Shaw are here replaced by young and truculent Blackshirts; and like the older man, evolving an idiosyncratic and cantankerous persona in inveterate contradiction with the fashions of the time.

That the parallel runs a little deeper than the role itself may be judged by *Tarr*, which is in this respect a virtual rewrite of *Man and Superman*, with its garrulous overintellectualized hero who succumbs to the invincible power of sex; by *The Childermass*, whose setting in the afterlife bears some striking similarities to the cosmological scheme of the "Don Juan in Hell" sequence of the same play and by *The Human Age*, which, with its reverse evolutionary perspective, is not without its affinities to the central themes of *Back to Methuselah*. To ask why Lewis did not simply become a fascist Shaw is to place ourselves squarely before the central issues of his work.

At the same time, Lewis was an internationalist, the most European and least insular of all the great contemporary British writers. He felt the impact of Dostoyevsky at a time when Gide was only just introducing the latter to the French-speaking world; and the Russian novelist's dramatization of the vagaries of individual consciousness clearly pave the way for the portrait of Kreisler, by general agreement the most remarkable psychological study in all of Lewis, with its grotesque self-revelatory outbursts. (Think only of the moment in which a sluggish and aroused Kreisler murmurs to his half-naked model, "Your

---

had been a young man when the Great War occurred, if he had studied painting and philosophy instead of economics and Ibsen, and if he had been more richly endowed with imagination, emotion, intellect and a few other things . . ." *Blasting and Bombardiering* (London: Eyre and Spottiswoode, 1937), p. 3.

arms are like bananas!" [*T*, 177], or of the climactic duel scene, when, seeing his adversary surreptitiously gulp tranquillizers, he shrieks, with all the ghastly peremptoriness of the winning child, "Give me one! . . . . I want a jujube. Ask Herr Soltyk! Tell him not to keep them for himself!" [*T*, 250]). In this sense, indeed, *Tarr*, with its double plot, and its twin heroes Tarr and Kreisler, may be described as a work in which a Shavian character contemplates the scandals of a Dostoyevskian social world. Lewis's politics, moreover, are profoundly marked by the book he called "the Bible of counter-revolution," Dostoyevsky's *The Possessed.*

Yet he was also one of the few great Western writers in recent times to have been deeply responsive to the German, as well as the Mediterranean, fact. He had studied in that country and understood it as something other than a symbol. In Kreisler he produced a German figure far more troubled and human than Lawrence's Prussian officer ("Tarr's sympathies were all with Kreisler. . . . an atavistic creature whom on the whole he preferred" [*T*, 267]). In Lewis' imagination, indeed, the German nation, as the pariah of European politics and the victim of Versailles, tends to figure the *id* rather than that repressive superego which the Prussian manner has generally connoted for foreigners. It is this German component which is no doubt as responsible as anything else for the deliberate cynicism of what is for Lewis as well as for Brecht the comedy of sex, the meaningless and exasperating bondage to desire:

> Ob sie wollen oder nicht,—sie sind bereit.
> Das ist die sexuelle Hörigkeit.

The pale Shavian situation thereby takes on something of the full-blooded and raucous joviality of *Baal:* it is a note which would have been inconceivable (for opposite reasons) either in the atmosphere of Anglo-Saxon prudishness or in the relatively culinary tradition of French sensuality;

and may serve as a useful corrective to present-day Reichian sexual optimism.

Lewis is indeed so keenly aware of these various national traditions that they constitute the very backdrop and organizational framework of the works written before World War I: the stories of *The Wild Body* and *Tarr* itself, with its portrait gallery of international Bohemia in the prewar City of Light. *Tarr* thus takes its place among the most characteristic monuments to the aristocratic-bohemian cosmopolitan and multilingual European culture of that period, whose most substantial expression is *The Magic Mountain* of Thomas Mann (1924). Such a juxtaposition reminds us that the use of national types projects an essentially allegorical mode of representation, in which the individual characters figure those more abstract national characteristics which are read as their inner essence. In its simplest form, that of the contemplation of a single foreign national essence alone, such allegory often serves as the instrument of cultural critique: thus Stendhal's heroic images of the Italian or the Spanish temperament are designed to humiliate the conformistic philistinism of the French business classes of his time by juxtaposing it with the *gestus* of a vanished Renaissance.

Yet where, as in *Tarr* or *Der Zauberberg*, the various national types find themselves grouped within a common ballroom or Grand Hotel, a more complex network of interrelations and collisions emerges, and with it a dialectically new and more complicated allegorical system. Now narrative meaning becomes relational, as momentary alliances develop and disintegrate. Fascinating apparitions—the Russo-German Anastasya of *Tarr*, the Polish Clawdia Chauchat of Thomas Mann's sanitorium—crisscross the field of force, leaving disarray behind them. Figures initially distant—Kreisler and the Englishman—slowly and with mutual wariness and distrust approach each other. Under these circumstances, allegory ceases to be that static decipherment of one-on-one correspondences with which it is still so often identified and opens up that specific and uniquely allegorical space between signifier and signified, in which "the signifier is what represents the subject for another signifier" (Lacan).[2] This is the sense in which the allegorical signified of such narratives is ultimately always World War I, or Apocalypse: not in any punctual prediction or reflection of this conflict as a chronological event, but rather as the ultimate conflictual "truth" of the sheer, mobile, shifting relationality of national types and of the older nation-states which are their content.

Hence the centrality of Kreisler himself, that "certain disquieting element" which is not without impunity introduced into the concourse of nations. Kreisler in Paris— that is the stiff and powerful, ungainly, explosive Prussian temperament in the throes of Culture, flinging "a man or a woman on to nine feet of canvas and [pummelling] them on it for a couple of hours, until they promised' to remain there or were incapable of moving" (*T*, 75). Even Kreisler in love tells the story of a national inferiority complex: paralyzed by the prospect of courting Anastasya, he catches fire at the chance of feeling jealousy, raging inwardly at the sight of her surreptitious conversations with the ill-fated Pole, Soltyk.

It is indeed around Soltyk that Kreisler's most turbid and volcanic emotions organize themselves: Soltyk, who has supplanted him as the borrower-in-chief of his friend Vokt's money; Soltyk, who is inexplicably able to murmur interminable small talk to Anastasya; Soltyk, above all, who with his "hereditary polish of manner," his "self-possession, his ready social accomplishment, depressed Kreisler: for it was not in his nature to respect those qualities, yet he felt they were what he always lacked" (*T*, 140).

Soltyk is in fact a virtual double of Kreisler, bearing a

---

2. Jacques Lacan, "Subversion du sujet et dialectique du désir," in *Écrits* (Paris: Seuil, 1966), p. 819. And compare this other dictum: "Only the relationship of one signifier to another signifier engenders the relationship of signifier to signified" (quoted in A. G. Wilden, *The Language of the Self* [Baltimore, Maryland: The Johns Hopkins Press, 1968], p. 239).

distant and mocking physical resemblance to the latter as though he represents some more prosperous and well-favored branch of the family, some far more successful second version, which can but reinforce the envy and resentment of the botched first draft. In cultural terms, then, Kreisler's fury reenacts the humiliation of Germany, not merely before the more sophisticated culture of the West, but even in the face of the Frenchified and Westernized culture of subject Poland as well. Unfortunately, in spite of the Pole's cultural polish, it is the German, along with his even more "alarming" Russian second, who has the real power. The duel scene (compare its anticlimactic equivalent in *Sentimental Education*) is thus a league of the strong against the weak, an acting out by the two great powers of their cultural marginalization, of which history's version is the sequence of Polish partitions, as well as the self-destructive sequels of the various Central and Eastern European war efforts. Lewis' psychopathology of Kreisler may thus be read as the figuration of that complex of German feelings which served as the ideological justification for the War, and as a virtually inexhaustible source of war enthusiasm, while the relational and allegorical structure of his narrative articulates (without conceptualizing it) that "combination of antagonistic principles. . . . that is the essence of imperialism" and that made 1914 inevitable.[3] On Lenin's view, indeed, the war of the nation-states is an ideological appearance ("nationality and fatherland as essential forms of the bourgeois system"[4]) which political praxis must both unmask as, and transform into, the reality of transnational civil war and class struggle: Lenin's program thereby corresponds exactly to the "break" in Lewis' own work and to the disintegration of his older national system.

3. V. I. Lenin, *Collected Works* (Moscow: Progress Publishers, 1961), Vol. 24, p. 465.
4. V. I. Lenin, *Collected Works* (Moscow: Progress Publishers, 1964), Vol. 21, p. 38.

What we must now investigate are the objective preconditions of this initial structure, which we will henceforth call "national allegory." The very unfamiliarity of this now outmoded narrative system suggests that as a formal possibility it is enabled by an objective situation whose modification once again excludes it. To understand the history of forms, as the ideologists of modernism do, as an autonomous dynamic of purely formal innovations, each of which is motivated by the will to replace an establishment form by a novelty at length superseded in its turn, is to think such modifications in an empty, cyclical and ultimately static way. From any point of view, however,—whether that of the formal possibilities themselves, or of their content—every great formal innovation is *determinate*, and reflects a situation that cannot immediately be assimilated to those which may precede or follow it.[5]

Meanwhile, it also seems useful to insist that the history of forms is not the only set of coordinates within which artistic production and innovation need to be understood. It should not be forgotten that the very concept of production itself—in wide currency today—entails a consequence which is less often explored, namely the requirement of a preexistent availability of certain specific raw materials, or what I have elsewhere called a specific "logic of content."[6] The question about the objective preconditions of a given form has the strategic advantage of allowing us to cut across the false problems of causality or "determinism": it does not program us into a situation

5. This is not to exclude more global analyses of the specific dynamic of such cultural and formal innovations, which is obviously closely related to the rhythm of capitalist production itself and which Barthes has described as "that purely formal process of the rotation of possibles which characterizes Fashion. . . . here *difference* is the motor, not of history, but of diachrony; history intervenes only when these micro-rhythms are perturbed. . . ." (Roland Barthes, *Essais critiques* [Paris: Seuil, 1964], p. 262).

6. Fredric Jameson, *Marxism and Form* (Princeton: Princeton University Press, 1971), pp. 327–331, and also pp. 164–169.

in which we find ourselves obliged to affirm the meaningless proposition that the verbal artifact *Tarr* was somehow "caused" by forces on the quite different levels of political history or socioeconomic organization. Rather, it directs our attention to the more sensible procedure of exploring those semantic and structural givens which are logically prior to this text and without which its emergence is inconceivable. This is of course the sense in which national allegory in general, and *Tarr* in particular, presuppose not merely the nation-state itself as the basic functional unit of world politics, but also the objective existence of a system of nation-states, the international diplomatic machinery of pre-World-War-I Europe which, originating in the 16th century, was dislocated in significant ways by the War and the Soviet Revolution.

This account of the preconditions of Lewis' novel is a very different proposition from interpretive statements which might take it as the "reflexion" of the European diplomatic system or see its violent content as betraying some "homology" with World War I. An analysis of the semantic and structural preconditions of a form is not a correspondence theory of art; nor do we mean to see national allegory as an afterimage given off by the international diplomatic system itself. Rather, like any form, it must be read as an instable and provisory solution to an aesthetic dilemma which is itself the manifestation of a social and historical contradiction.

Thus, national allegory should be understood as a formal attempt to bridge the increasing gap between the existential data of everyday life within a given nation-state and the structural tendency of monopoly capital to develop on a worldwide, essentially transnational scale. Nineteenth-century or "classical" realism presupposed the relative intelligibility and self-sufficiency of the national experience from within, a coherence in its social life such that the narrative of the destinies of its individual citizens can be expected to achieve formal completeness. It is this formal possibility which the pan-European allegory of *Tarr* now calls into question, implying the increasing inability of English life to furnish the raw materials for an intelligible narrative code. Tarr himself, with his observer's aloofness from his setting, in this respect dramatizes the security of the liberal and counterrevolutionary class compromise of the British tradition from the seething and politicized history of the continental states. Yet this security is abstract: at the very same moment, owing to its momentary industrial and naval supremacy, the British Empire is inextricably and structurally involved in and dependent on the outside world—whence the rather different, more properly colonial allegory of a novel like Forster's *Passage to India*. Thus the lived experience of the British situation is domestic, while its structural intelligibility is international: it is from this dilemma that *Tarr* as an aesthetic totality seeks to deliver itself.[7]

We have not done with national allegory, however, when we have specified the conditions for its emergence as a narrative system. Once in place, such a system has a kind of objectivity about it, and wins a semiautonomy as a cultural structure which can then know an unforeseeable history in its own right, as an object cut adrift from its originating situation and "freed" for the alienation of a host of quite different signifiying functions and uses, whose content rushes in to invest it. This is the point, then, at which we mark the transformation of national allegory into what J. F. Lyotard has called a *libidinal apparatus*, an empty form or structural matrix in which a charge of free-floating and inchoate fantasy—both ideological and psychoanalytic—can suddenly crystallize, and find the articulated figuration essential for its social actuality and psychic effectivity.

In the case of *Tarr*, we will suggest that the empty ma-

---

7. See for an inventory of the formal consequences of this "break" in English literature, Terry Eagleton's *Exiles and Emigres* (New York: Schocken, 1970): "The process of grasping any culture as a whole, of discerning its essential forms and directions, is always, needless to say, an acutely difficult task; but that difficulty seems significantly exacerbated in modern English society" (p. 221).

trix of national allegory is then immediately seized on by hitherto unformulable impulses which invest its structural positions and, transforming the whole narrative system into a virtual allegory of the fragmented psyche itself, now reach back to overdetermine the resonance of this now increasingly layered text. The history of Freud's own work may be invoked as testimony for such a process of figuration and reinvestment or overdetermination: not only are the Freudian models allegories, they can also be shown to depend for their figural expression on elaborate and preexisting representations of the topography of the city and the dynamics of the political state. This urban and civil "apparatus"—often loosely referred to as a Freudian "metaphor"—is the objective precondition for Freud's representation of the psyche, and is thus at one with the very "discovery" of the unconscious itself, which may now be seen to have presupposed the objective development— the industrialization, the social stratification and class polarization, the complex division of labor—of the late Victorian city. Nor is the post-War transformation of this properly Freudian "libidinal apparatus" into the "energy model" of the rivalry of Eros and Thanatos without striking similarities to the "break" in Lewis' work which is contemporaneous with it.[8]

At this point, then, we may rewrite everything we have said about the national dynamics of *Tarr* in terms of this new, second-level psychic allegory. In the new system, Tarr, the observing consciousness, the artist as detached as possible from life and sex, the rational mind attempting to confine itself to the pure, atemporal realm of art, is now, in his signifying opposition to the dourly instinctual Kreisler, positioned as a hypertrophied ego for whom the

8. After the early *Project for a Scientific Psychology* (1895), at least three distinct models of the psyche coexist in Freud's work: the topographical (Unconscious, Preconscious, Conscious); the economic (Ego, Id, Superego); and the late hypothesis of the death wish, the dualism of Eros and Thanatos, here henceforth designated as the energy model.

break with Bertha marks an attempt to flee the organic itself:

> God was man: the woman was a lower form of life. Everything started female and so continued: a jellyish diffuseness spread itself and gaped upon all the beds and bas-fonds of everything: above a certain level sex disappeared, just as in highly-organized sensualism sex vanishes. On the other hand *everything* beneath that line was female . . . He enumerated acquaintances palpably below that absolute line: a lack of energy, permanently mesmeric state, almost purely emotional, they all displayed it, they were true 'women'. That line had been crossed by Anastasya: he would not be a pervert because he had slept with her, but more than that would be peculiar.
>
> (*T*, 293–294)

It should be noted that while women, the organic, and sex itself are here all identified within a mythic, clearly negative term, there is no correlative celebration of the male principle. The peculiarity of Lewis' sexual ideology is that, while openly misogynist, and sexist in the obvious senses of the word, it is not for all that phallocentric. The positive term which logically corresponds to the negative one of the female principle is not the male, as in D. H. Lawrence, but rather art, which is not the place of a subject, masculine or otherwise, but rather impersonal and inhuman, or, as Lewis liked to say, "dead," spatial rather than temporal and existential:

> Deadness is the first condition of art. The armoured hide of the hippopotamus, the shell of the tortoise, feathers and machinery, you may put in one camp; naked pulsing and moving of the soft inside of life— along with the elasticity of movement and consciousness—that goes in the opposite camp. Deadness is the first condition for art: the second is absence of soul, in the human and sentimental sense. With the statue its lines and masses are its soul, no restless inflammable ego is imagined for its interior: it has *no inside:* good art must have no inside: that is capital. (*T*, 279–280)

This, which is virtually the letter of what will later become Lewis' own aesthetic program—called *satire*—is here still the mere opinion of one of his characters: the coincidence of authorial value with Tarr's structural position as a character within the novel marks him as the first and last fully positive figure in Lewis' work, at the same time that it virtually excludes him from the narrative itself. In his fashion, indeed, Tarr attempts to realize the Shavian superman and to project an almost evolutionary mutation of the species, from which the artist can emerge from the latter's organic necessity. Yet if he succeeds, he fails; for of such an artist, no story can henceforth be told, and the narrative of Tarr must very quickly give place to a quite different one, namely that of Kreisler.

The character of Tarr can therefore not serve as a vehicle for the celebration of some mythic phallocentric value. Yet the point can be made in a different way by observing that the male axis of this narrative—the agon between Tarr and Kreisler—is itself structurally incomplete, and thereby condemned to an oscillation which must exclude even that imaginary synthesis of the autonomous bourgeois individual on which the phallocentric ideology is necessarily based. Kreisler is clearly enough the place of the instincts, of a pathological regression or drop in the "niveau" of consciousness which opens it to the wildest impulses from across this undefended frontier, from the blind spasms of schizophrenic caprice all the way to outright aggressivity and rape. Yet the terms of this symbolic coding are essentially dictated by Tarr's position, from the perspective of an ego seeking to declare its independence from organic life. This is to say that, unlike Freud's topographic model, the psychic system of *Tarr* knows no superego; the binary agon lacks that third term which allowed Freud to postulate a unified psyche. The superego was indeed the mechanism that permitted Freud to write a *history* of psychic life, and to grasp and interpret all those complex and indirect, substitute investments of desire which lie between the empty conscious subject and the archaic, infantile id. Yet Lewis' narrative is locked into this static binary opposition in much the same way that his national allegory is paralyzed by the conception of nation-states (rather than the more genuinely historical dynamic of class antagonism) as the equivalent subjects of a history which can thus only end in catastrophe.

We may now block out the narrative system of *Tarr* along the lines of Greimas' semiotic rectangle:[9]

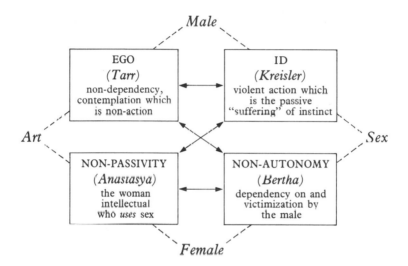

Such a model would appear to justify a conventional structural analysis of the novel as the transformation of this system into an exchange mechanism by which some final illusion of harmony, some final "imaginary" solution of the contradiction it articulates, can be generated. From Tarr's point of view, the events of the novel mainly serve

9. The rectangle is the representation of a binary opposition (two contraries), along with the simple negations (or contradictories) of both terms (the so-called sub-contraries), plus the various possible combinations of these terms, most notably the "complex term" (ideal synthesis of the two contraries) and the "neutral" term (ideal synthesis of the two sub-contraries). See A. J. Greimas and François Rastier, "The Interaction of Semiotic Constraints" (Yale French Studies, No. 41 [1968], pp. 86–105); and Frédéric Nef, ed., *Structures élémentaires de la signification* (Brussels: Editions Complexe, 1976); and see also my *Prison-House of Language* (Princeton: Princeton University Press, 1972), pp. 162–168.

to resolve a pressing personal dilemma: how to get rid of the importunate Bertha. On the mimetic level, then, his difficulties involve nothing more than a reluctance to wound someone for whom he has no respect: we have already seen, however, that the break with Bertha is the allegorical figure of a release from the organic itself.

This is the point at which the person and the structural position of Kreisler intervene. Kreisler's destiny, acted out, *frees* Tarr: such is at least the "solution" that could be expected by the operation of a symbolic exchange within the narrative. What is exchanged first and foremost are evidently the women characters: Tarr receives the object of Kreisler's infatuation (Anastasya), thus obligating the latter to take Bertha in return. Kreisler's affair with Bertha, if it can be called that, then releases Tarr from his obligations to her, at the same time that the violence with which she is possessed symbolically assauges the latent hostilities developed by the unhappy liaison. Anastasya is, however, unlike Bertha, Tarr's intellectual equal, so that the affair with her already constitutes an initial liberation from the body as such ("but more than that would be peculiar"). Meanwhile, to see Kreisler as Tarr's life-surrogate is to be able to grasp the peculiarly *fin de siècle* or Gidean flourish of Tarr's concluding gesture: to marry Bertha *because* she bears the dead Kreisler's child amounts to a ratification of the structural substitution, and a reciprocal repayment for Kreisler's liberation of Tarr himself.

This is, however, not a satisfactory resolution to the contradiction or ideological closure in which the narrative found itself, for its fundamental terms, its stark and wellnigh mythic oppositions, admit of no structural solution. Tarr himself draws the moral of the story with the following interpretation of Kreisler's self-destructive destiny:

> I believe that all the fuss he made was an attempt to get out of Art back into Life again. He was like a fish floundering about who had got into the wrong tank. *Back into sex* I think would describe where he wanted

to get to: he was doing his best to get back into sex
again out of a little puddle of art where he felt he was
gradually expiring. He was an art-student without
any talent you see, so the poor devil was leading a
slovenly meaningless existence like thousands of
others in the same case. He was very hard up also.
The sex-instinct of the average sensual man had
become perverted into a false channel. Put it the
other way round and say his art instinct had been
rooted out of sex, where it was useful, and naturally
flourished, and had been exalted into a department
by itself, where it bungled. The nearest the general
run get to art is *Action:* sex is their form of art: the
battle for existence is their picture. The moment they
think or *dream* they develop an immense weight of
cheap stagnating passion. Art, in the hands of the
second-rate, is a curse, it is on a par with 'freedom' —
but we are not allowed to say *second-rate* are
we—he grinned—in the midst of a democracy!
particularly such a 'cultivated' one as this! But if
you are forbidden to say *second-rate,* why then you
must leave behind you all good sense—*nothing* can
be discussed at all if you can't say *second-rate!*

(*T,* 281–282)

The later Lewis would have much to say about *second-rate*
indeed; but *Tarr* is still in this sense a prepolitical novel,
and the emergence of this characteristic motif here is
merely anticipatory. To rewrite the opposition between
Tarr and Kreisler in terms of the genius or strong personality and the average mediocrity of "mass man" will, as we
shall see shortly, involve a complete overhaul and restructuration of Lewis' narrative apparatus. For the moment, the unexpected appearance of the political and
ideological motif in *Tarr* signals the incapacity of this system to resolve itself in its own terms. We have already
shown that the triumph of the term marked "Art" would
at once position Tarr outside the narrative and exclude
him from the world of action and events. Kreisler's slovenly end obscures the equally unsatisfactory consequences
of the triumph of the sexual term, which can be described

as the dreary and cyclical repetition of the organic, a meaningless succession of sex acts which are as surely beyond history or narrative as the realm of art itself. This is indeed, it seems to me, the only way to read the novel's enigmatic, unresolved final paragraph, which enumerates the unfamiliar names of Tarr's future lovers:

> Two years after the birth of the child, Mrs. Tarr [Bertha] divorced him: she then married an eye-doctor and lived with a brooding severity in his company and that of her only child.
>
> Tarr and Anastasya did not marry. They had no children. Tarr, however, had three children by a lady of the name of Rose Fawcett, who consoled him eventually for the splendours of his "perfect woman". But yet beyond the dim though solid figure of Rose Fawcett, another rises. This one represents the swing back of the pendulum once more to the swagger side. The cheerless and stodgy absurdity of Rose Fawcett required as compensation the painted, fine and enquiring face of Prism Dirkes. (*T*, 299)

The implication is not merely that the Shavian superman has failed and sunk back into "Life" and "Sex," into the organic; the narrative has failed also, continuing for a few anticlimactic bars to sound the appropriate melodies and give the obligatory information about the characters' afterlife. Yet these characters are not subjects, and their later "histories" are structurally irrelevant: the peculiar nonfunctionality of this coda or narrative recapitulation now returns to cast some doubt on the narrative that left it thus hanging there, like a stray but terminal wrong note.

In the twenties, Wyndham Lewis leaves the Shavian-Dostoyevskian novel behind him, and a new narrative apparatus—called *satire*—makes a stupefying and unexpected appearance in his work. Lewis himself dates this fundamental "break," both in the world and in his own artistic practice, from the British General Strike of 1926 (depicted in the closing pages of *The Apes of God*). Yet it is clear that this emblematic and punctual event, like all extreme moments of social and protorevolutionary polarization, had the effect of articulating as explicitly political and ideological positions a relationship to changes in the world already long since in place. We have already suggested that the War, with its demolition of the older diplomatic system of the nation states, put an end to national allegory, and with it, to the libidinal apparatus we have examined in *Tarr*. What now emerged was less visible as the nascent primacy of the new superstates, nor even as the world system of multinational capitalism, whose crises were at that time more evident than its dynamic and its capacity for expansion: what Lewis' work registers is above all the dramatic appearance of the great postnational ideologies of Communism and Fascism. Now parties rather than nation-states are the active categories of historical and political life, which plays itself out in forces that cut across the old national boundary lines. In this new world, not England and Germany, Spain or Poland, but rather Communism and Fascism are the principal agents and "subjects" of history (to this list, Lewis will after World War II add the supplementary forces of tradition—essentially Roman Catholicism—and nonideological power or corrupt *Realpolitik* in the person of the Bailiff).

This new "energy model" now disrupts the grid of the older national allegory just as surely as Freud's conception of the eternal forces of Eros and Thanatos explodes the older psychic topologies. The most accessible symptom of this momentous break in Lewis' work will be the eclipse of the place of the subject or ego—the disappearance of the locus of Tarr himself, the placeless observer "out of life and out of sex" who now finds himself irresistibly politicized, drawn into the force field of the ideologies and the instincts and transformed beyond recognition. Yet his opposite number, Kreisler, the place of archaic regression, must also thereby vanish, his uncontrollable impulses and aggressivity now released as unbound, transindividual forces objectively present in the new social world itself. Not the novelist's private and public obsessions, however, but rather the very structure of the reality in which they achieve figuration has been decisively modified.

6/
"THE DISSOLVING BODY OF GOD'S CHIMAERA"

Our only terra firma in a boiling and shifting world is, after all, our 'self'. That must cohere for us to be capable at all of behaving in any way but as mirror-images of alien realities, or as the most helpless and lowest organisms, as worms or sponges. I have said to myself that I will fix my attention upon those things that have most meaning for me. All that seems to me to contradict or threaten those things I will do my best to modify or to defeat, and whatever I see that favours and agrees with those things I will support and do my best to strengthen. In consequence, I shall certainly be guilty of injustice, the heraclitean 'injustice of the opposites'. But how can we evade our destiny of becoming 'an opposite', except by becoming some grey mixture, that is in reality just nothing at all?

Time and Western Man

HE FIRST CONSEQUENCES OF THIS "break" in Lewis' formal development, and of the problematization of the subject that accompanies it, will be a shift in the literal level of the text, or, to put it a different way, a displacement in the way characters (and reader) project its "reality." In *Tarr,* as we have seen, the actors suffer from unpredictable lapses and contractions of their life-world, traverse strange sleepwalking stretches in which their sense of external reality is weakened to its most tenuous. Yet in spite of the expressionistic mode of representation, these states are still essentially conceived as psychological phenomena: it is the characters who at such moments lose touch with a reality and a world the stability of which is, however, never itself called into question. The allegorical reading operations which we have already analyzed tend, indeed, to determine a reconstruction of the missing literal level by the reader. In the

post-World-War-I narratives, however, life itself becomes unreal, and human beings are represented as virtual puppets, enjoying a spasmodic and degraded existence, their bodies jerkily obedient to the first principles of positivist physiology, while their minds function as textbook illustrations of the mechanisms of behavioristic and Pavlovian laws. Paradoxically, the new reading operations demanded by such texts reverse the earlier process of reconstruction. Now stability is no longer to be found in some literal level of the characters' *Umwelt* or situation; yet we are not for all that asked to center a new literal level within the subject itself, of which experience would then become the mere hallucinatory projection. Rather, the structure of the pseudocouple is inserted between these two options (which are something like a philosophical realism and idealism on the narrative level respectively) such that both subject and object poles are held open and suspended.

Thus preoccupations which are still secondary motifs in *Tarr* or *The Wild Body* become central in the post-War libidinal apparatus. With *The Childermass,* we register a change from the older thematic content and official philosophical issues (Art vs. Sex) to an overtly "philosophical" form which explicitly raises questions about the nature of the personality or of individuality. *The Childermass* (and the entire *Human Age* of which it is a part) stages something like a search for the ego, for the unifying principle of some autonomous, central subject, at the same time exploring the effects of the systematic dispersal of psychic unity by various historical agencies, of which at present we have only noted that of the metonymic fission of Lewis' style.

Yet in the early works, even where the relationship of the machine to the individual subject is grasped as a kind of decentering, this dissolution of individuality is not always staged negatively, as the loss, nightmare, or malign enchantment which it will shortly become. For a brief moment, indeed, the mechanical stands as the figure for the collective, and an unrealized option or tendency in Lewis' first narratives lingers with sympathy on "the fascinating imbecility of the creaking men machines, that some little restaurant or fishing boat works" (*SH,* 67). The tentative "essays in a new human logic" constituted by the stories and sketches of *The Wild Body* thus begin to abstract a new narrative system from the post-individualistic realities of collective work and group *praxis,* at least to the degree to which the latter can be articulated and given figuration by the central working mechanism or machine itself:

> A man is made drunk with his boat or restaurant as
> he is with a merry-go-round: only it is the staid,
> everyday drunkenness of the normal real, not easy
> always to detect. We can all see the ascendance a
> 'carousel' has on men, driving them into a set narrow
> intoxication. The wheel at Carisbrooke imposes a set
> of movements upon the donkey inside it, in drawing
> water from the well, that it is easy to grasp. But in
> the case of a hotel or fishing boat, for instance, the
> complexity of the rhythmic scheme is so great that it
> passes as open and untrammeled life. This subtle and
> wider mechanism merges, for the spectator, in the
> general variety of nature. Yet we have in most lives
> the spectacle of a pattern as circumscribed and com-
> plete as a theorem of Euclid. . . . These intricately
> moving bobbins are all subject to a set of objects or to
> one in particular. (*SH,* 67-68)

The satiric tone—workers as cogs or "bobbins," as "puppets," mere "shadows of energy, not living beings" whose "mechanism is a logical structure" (*SH,* 69)—should not distract us from the great anticipatory interest of these sketches as approaches to the dynamics of group praxis, of the kind studied most notably in Sartre's *Critique of Dialectical Reason* (1960)[1]; and as experiments with the

1. Jean-Paul Sartre, *Critique of Dialectical Reason* (London: New Left Books, 1976), pp. 345–404; and see for a summary my *Marxism and Form* (Princeton: Princeton University Press, 1971), pp. 247–257.

representation of a collective or postindividualistic content of which until now only certain filmic languages (Dziga Vertov's *Man with the Movie Camera* is the most notable example) have given us a glimpse.

The exploration of this narrative option would by its own inner logic and momentum have ended up positioning Lewis squarely on the Left. His abandonment of such experiments may thus be understood in the light of a more fundamental ideological choice, and in particular of his lifelong resistance to Marxism. Yet the experience of World War I is surely also not without some decisive effect on the exploration of the representational possibilities of the "collective machine." The War marks indeed a kind of grisly climax to this relationship of individuals to vast impersonal and technological mechanisms which can no longer be celebrated joyously. Meanwhile, the criminal bloodletting of the trenches, and the callousness with which the various ruling classes flung their populations into the deadly fire of the machine gun, now transform the "masses" from the functional parts of a collective mechanism into its mere passive victims and martyrs.

The enormity of the transformation may be measured by the reappearance of this anonymous working population in *The Childermass,* where they have become the insubstantial "peons," Dante's "trimmers," the "masses of personalities whom God, having created them, is unable to destroy, but who are not distinct enough to remain more than what you see. Indistinct ideas, don't you know" (*CM,* 28):

> Satters in the dirty mirror of the fog sees a hundred images, in the aggregate, sometimes as few as twenty, it depends if his gaze is steadfast. Here and there their surfaces collapse altogether as his eyes fall upon them, the whole appearance vanishes, the man is gone. But as the pressure withdraws of the full-blown human glance the shadow reassembles, in the same stark posture, every way as before, at the same spot—obliquely he is able to observe it coming back

jerkily into position. One figure is fainter than any of
the rest, he is a thin and shabby mustard yellow, in
colouring a flat daguerrotype or one of the personnel
of a pre-war film, split tarnished and transparent
from travel and barter. He comes and goes; sometimes he is there, then he flickers out. He is a tall
man of no occupation, in the foreground. He falls
like a yellow smear upon one much firmer than himself behind, or invades him like a rusty putrefaction,
but never blots out the stronger person.   (*CM*, 22)

The relationship of these intermittent figures to the equally
abstract painterly gaze which tends to measure their unreality by dissolving them is evidently a constitutive dialectic which we will want to explore further, and which
betrays and dramatizes the aggressive and problematic
connection between the satirist and his victims.

For the moment, what must be stressed is the way in
which the new vision displaces the crisis of the self, and,
by discrediting these masses of what Tarr called the
"second-rate," generates the mirage of a positive counter-
term which was not yet present in the earlier apparatus,
namely the locus and the ideological valorization of the
"strong personality" itself. Now the attention of characters
and reader alike is directed to the pursuit of this ideal, and
the dead are ultimately judged on the degree of individual
reality, or "personality," they have managed to acquire in
life.

The Bailiff's recommendation for somewhat weaker
individuals is to be sure not altogether honest:

Those who can combine should do so—that is the
rule: it saves time. Also such combinations ensure the
maximum effect of reality—I have known cases of a
man being completely restored to his true and
essential identity after meeting an old friend it's most
valuable it's the tip we always give the newcomer,
dig out the old pal there's nothing like it. But in no
case should the group be too large. These conditions
observed, we shall then carefully note your points
of difference and your claim to personal survival.

(*CM*, 137)

The negative qualification is the key to this strategy: explicitly beyond the pale are those groups which are "too large," or in other words the expression of the realities of social class itself, as they are embodied in mass political parties and ideological movements of the type created by the Bailiff's adversary, Hyperides (the representative of revolutionary fascism). In fact, what the Bailiff is here proposing—in the form of a properly "diabolical" temptation—is the constitution of what we have already called the pseudocouple, the makeshift dependency and mutual reinforcement of two damaged subjects.

Nor do the lapses in being suffered by the "stronger" personalities undermine the now dominant ideological value of individual identity; if anything, they merely tend to reconfirm it and to perpetuate its centrality for the characters:

> Pullman looks up. Satters gazes into a sallow vacant mask, on which lines of sour malice are disappearing, till it is blank and elementary, in fact the face of a clay doll.
>   'Why, you are a peon!' Satters cries pointedly, clapping his hands.
>   Pullman recovers at his cry, and his face, with muscular initiative, shrinks as though in the grip of a colossal sneeze. The screwed-up cuticle is a pinched blister of a head-piece: it unclenches, and the normal Pullman-mask emerges, but still sallow, battered, and stiff-lipped. (*CM*, 37)

The ideal of the "strong personality"—too complex to be resumed under the current term of "elitism"—is in fact the central organizational category of Lewis' mature ideology, and the primary "value" from which are generated all those more provocative, yet structurally derivative ideological motifs and obsessions of racism and sexism, the attack on the Youth Cult, the disgust with parliamentary democracy, the satiric aesthetic of Otherness, the violent polemic and moral stance of the didactic works, the momentary infatuation with Nazism as well as the implacable repudiation of Marxism.

Yet, as we have suggested in our Prologue, ideology is not a *Weltanschauung,* not a coherent system of ideas, but rather the desperate response to a contradictory situation. The notion of the "strong personality" in Lewis is then not to be read as a "belief," a conceptual value or conviction, but rather as a symbolic act in its own right, which has then taken on the reified appearance of a "thought" or an "opinion." We can therefore only do justice to the peculiar structure of the phenomenon of ideology—something like a "neurotically denied" unit of theory and practice, in which a pseudothought can be shown to have the disguised but concrete function of signifying group adhesion and designating the place of a properly group praxis[2] —by reconstructing the social and historical situation in terms of which its symbolic value as an act can be grasped.

This situation has already very abstractly been characterized as the crisis of the subject; yet even this term now requires further specification in order to forestall the impression that we have to do here with some purely psychological category. In fact, the determination of the individual subject is an objective and historical process which must be approached on three distinct levels: (1) the linguistic, in which the individual subject is determined by language structures, as the subject of enunciation, or the shifter, and on the narrative level, as the effect of categories like the literary character, or point of view, or the more purely operational procedures of the reader of the schizophrenic "text"; (2) the psychoanalytic, in which the "existential experience" of consciousness is decentered and deconstructed as the constituted "effect" of a structure whose dynamics are comprehensible only in terms of the hypothesis of an Unconscious; (3) the legal or juridical, in

2. Ibid., p. 300, n. 88: "The essence of racism, in effect, is that it is not a system of thoughts which might be false or pernicious . . . *It is not a thought at all* . . . Racism is the colonial interest lived as a link of all the colonialists of the colony through the serial flight of alternity . . . as material exigencies of language . . . addressed to colonists as members of a series and *signifying* them as colonialists both in their own eyes and in those of others, in the unity of a gathering."

which the "autonomy" of the bourgeois subject is generated by the "equality"—or rather, the sheer equivalence—of the market system and by the "freedom" to sell your own labor-power.

A "crisis" of the type we are positing in Lewis' work must thus be identified on all three of these levels, as a perturbation of representational categories, which releases free-floating psychic impulses at the same time that it expresses the social and occupational anxieties of a determinate, historically threatened class fraction. A first thematic approach to this historical crisis can be made by way of a whole complex of motifs and preoccupations which the biographical Lewis (or his various journalistic personae) shared with a generation of post-War Western European intellectuals.

Here a host of related contemporary discussions and reactions allow us to identify Lewis' personal articulation of the crisis of the subject in terms of the widespread and relatively banal perception of the levelling effects of industrial society and the emergence of what are called "the masses," frighteningly standardized by the intensification of the media, the growth of technology, and the setting in place of circuits of mechanical transportation and circulation. The overt political and social "theories" to which this experience gave rise throughout the 1920's and 30's will be examined in the next chapter: here we are concerned with the ways in which such alarmed perceptions are articulated in narratives which can also be seen as ways of managing and defusing them.

A formal example from an earlier stage in this process of what is sometimes euphemistically called "modernization" may clarify this particular problematic before we examine Lewis' work in its terms. The emergence of naturalism as a formal innovation and a determinate narrative apparatus is indeed extremely suggestive as to the way in which a modification in aesthetic technique has a socially and ideologically symbolic value. Naturalism, along with its breakdown products such as the bestseller, has become institutionalized and "naturalized" for us as a "realistic" mimesis of common sense reality. Yet its representational structures are far more complex and contradictory, and project the coexistence and superposition of two distinct narrative modes: the stream-of-consciousness or point-of-view *internal* rendering of a character which is however globally conceived *from without,* as a reified destiny, as the external Otherness of the proletarian, or the marginal, or the victim of heredity. This double focus allows the narrative to express, but at the same time to assuage, the central social anxiety of its bourgeois readership, namely the terror of *déclassement* and of proletarianization, the nightmare of slipping back down the social ladder, losing your painfully won savings and business and professional status and sinking into a misery you only know from without, as the squalor of proletarian neighborhoods and the drunken hebetude of workers or the brutish mutism of a sullen peasantry. The naturalist apparatus gives this fantasy imaginative content, by allowing its readership to project itself into such alien experiences as those of the worker or the prostitute, the beggar or the criminal; yet the molar reification of this experience—not, like "our own" a freedom and an open present, but rather a determinism and a destiny fatally programmed in advance—then comfortably reassures the reader as to his or her fundamental difference and reconfirms the security of the middle-class surroundings in which the naturalist novel is read.

By the time of Lewis, however, even this still relatively secure vantage point has disappeared under the impact of inflation, the War Debt, and economic crisis, and the new urban technology which seems to efface the safe frontier between the life of the masses and the life of the petty bourgeoisie. Indeed, in proportion to the levelling of such material articulations of class difference, the bourgeois subject experiences itself as an increasingly isolated monad confronted with an anonymous and faceless multitude:

> Unreal City,
> Under the brown fog of a winter dawn,
> A crowd flowed over London Bridge, so many,
> I had not thought death had undone so many.

The class anxiety that informed naturalism persists but is no longer articulated in anything resembling class terms: the petty bourgeois subjects of the 1920's do not live it as the terror of falling into a social space which is radically Other, but rather as an obscure sense that their own social space is contracting all around them, that soon they will have no structural or institutional place of their own, without being able to give any concrete expression to the unknown future that may lie beyond this fateful development. Here, if anywhere, we may identify the ultimate source of Lewis' anti-Marxism, and more generally, of the refusal of socialism which determines the recontainment of socialist impulses in protofascism: socialism or communism is fantasized as the completion of this process of levelling, and as the definitive loss of even this embattled and precarious, historically threatened status to which the petty bourgeois subject desperately clings.[3]

That this experience is a constant in Lewis may be demonstrated by a post-World-War-II version of those now dated and conventional 20's and 30's denunciations of "mass man" of which so many examples can be found throughout his works. Now, however, Pullman's first shocked impressions of the Magnetic City recapitulate a new referent, Mr. Atlee's Welfare State, which the stories of *Rotting Hill* (1952) then identify in more explicit or realistic form:

> 'Is this Heaven?' Pullman at last blankly inquired of the air. It reminded him of Barcelona. This, like the

---

3. According to J. P. Stern, in his interesting book *Hitler: The Führer and the People* (Berkeley and Los Angeles: University of California Press, 1975), this is also the situation that dictated the terms of Hitler's own political conversion: "What divided him from socialism was the most tenaciously held and desperate of social attitudes, the petit-bourgeois fear of *déclassement*" (58).

> Rambla, was a tree-lined avenue with huge pave-
> ments, across which cafes thrust hundreds of tables
> and chairs, to the edge of the gutter. Thousands of
> people overflowed the cafe terraces. . . . As they
> began to pass the lines of tables nearest the road,
> faces came into view. They were the faces of non-
> entities; this humanity was alarmingly sub-normal,
> all pig-eye or owlish vacuity. Was this a population
> of idiots—astonishingly well-dressed; as noticeably as
> the contemporary English are seedy or 'utility' clad?
> Yet this selective mediocrity laughed abnormally, and
> its voice was high. . . . Something that struck one
> about all these people was that their faces were
> youthful. They were such as a young man would get
> if he had been young for a very long time, until the
> skin had come to look like parchment.
>
> (*MG*, 14–15, 17)

The equally momentous changes wrought in British society by World War II do not have the same effect on Lewis'
narrative system as the "break" of the First World War,
because of the terms in which his mature cultural critique
had been conceived. His was not the conventional denunciation of science, rationalization, and technology, but was
rather formulated as an immanent social diagnosis whose
motifs (or obsessions)—in particular, the increasing stress
on youth and young people, the rise of feminism, and the
spread of homosexuality—could with little effort be imag-
inatively readapted to the quite different atmosphere of
British social democracy.

Meanwhile, the perspective of the monadic subject, the
placeless isolated observing eye, which registers these developments as a global social phenomenon and as a mass of
undifferentiated "peons" or moronic consumers, now generates a causal explanation in the form of a new narrative
axis: if this mindless degeneration has been visited on an
entire society, it can only be the result of some malignant
agency. Thus conspiracy theory and the place of the
Enemy make their appearance in the person of the Bailiff,
who, it is explained to Pullman, "is entirely responsible for

the degraded type of mannikin which swarms in this city" (*MG*, 121). With this emergence of the negative, diabolical term, the intrigue and the very title of *The Human Age* is given, as the unmasking of a vast cosmological plot by the *Zeitgeist* to reduce strong personalities (whether those of angels or of human "genius") to the level of the mediocre and the mindlessly standardized.

With this anxiety we are at the very heart of Lewis' ideological system. That its official positions are less important than the dilemmas or contradictions which they address may be judged by their antithetical yet symmetrical variants in the ideology of T. S. Eliot (for whom Maurras' *Action française* takes the place of Mussolini for Pound, or Hitler for Lewis). Eliot's aesthetic and political neoclassicism would seem, indeed, to foresee quite different solutions to the "problem" of the personality than that of Lewis: "The progress of an artist is a continual self-sacrifice, a continual extinction of personality. . . . Poetry is not a turning loose of emotion, but an escape from emotion; it is not the expression of personality, but an escape from personality. But, of course, only those who have personality and emotions know what it means to want to escape from these things."[4] Yet, as the political affinities between the two positions suggest, both the defense of individualism and the strong personality against the inroads of the masses, and the abdication of the personality to the security of spiritual and temporal authority remain locked into the categories of the individual subject, and, mere ideological permutations of the same underlying system, stand as complementary responses to the same fundamental experience of *anomie*.

It now remains to describe this underlying system, which we have already characterized, in contrast with the

---

4. T. S. Eliot, *Selected Essays* (New York: Harcourt, Brace, 1950), pp. 7, 10–11. And see, on Lewis' relationship to contemporary "neoclassical" political thought, Geoffrey Wagner, *Wyndham Lewis: A Portrait of the Artist as the Enemy* (New Haven: Yale University Press, 1957), pp. 90–101.

psychic model of *Tarr*, as an "energy" model in which forces, rather than topological positions and psychic "functions," become the essential terms. The logic of an energy model lies in its quantification of older qualitative components; in its attempt to reduce the heterogeneous substances and impulses of older kinds of models to the unified plus/minus system of a single force, whose increments then determine the variety and the conflicts of the world of phenomenal appearance. We would therefore expect, in such a model, to witness the dissolution of those rather mythic or alchemical dualisms which in *Tarr* took the form of the opposition between "Sex" and "Art," or between "Male" and "Female." The possibilities of such a transformation are, however, already present in *Tarr* itself, yet in a secondary or subordinate, rather than a dominant, position. Indeed, a reexamination of the semiotic rectangle we have constructed for *Tarr* shows that, while the dominant antinomy or binary opposition—between ego and id, or Tarr and Kreisler—is unresolvable or unassimilable as such, the same cannot be said for the subcontraries, the places of Bertha and Anastasya, which are articulated in terms of weakness and strength. To put it another way, the opposition between Tarr and Kreisler can in no way be rewritten as the opposition between the "strong personality" and the weak one—Kreisler is in that sense the very opposite of the later trimmer or peon—but the opposition between Anastasya and Bertha is very explicitly a juxtaposition between the strong and the weak or dependent woman.

This new "code" of strength, in which "weakness" is not an opposite term but a mere privation, now in the new energy model of the later works becomes the dominant and discredits all of the previous oppositions, "Male" and "Female" just as fully as "Sex" and "Art." If it is in this sense a "solution," however—the older binary terms now being replaced by a single, quasi-measurable concept of force—it is no less contradictory as an ideology, no less an antinomy for the conceptual, as well as the narrative, mind. For one thing, the place of that supreme value—intelligence—which it was the function of the new ideology preeminently to defend, is by no means clear: if intelligence is the same as strength, then there would be no need to defend it in the first place. (The Nietzschean vindication of strength, undone by the ruses of the weak and by their ideology of charity and self-sacrifice, involves analogous paradoxes.)

In *The Human Age*, indeed, intelligence unexpected comes to be identified as "a compensation for our weakness. . . . We are helpless, powerless mites of intelligence" (*MG*, 140). Thereby identified with the fragility of human life as such, intelligence generates an opposite which is a plenitude in its own right, and quite different from the mindless vacuity of the peons or of the Bailiff's emasculated subjects: this strange new term is that of the superhuman, or of the angelic nature, a vitalistic "natural" force which must be seen as *mindless* from the point of view of human weakness:

> For *me* the archangel nicknamed by you and your
> friends 'Padishah' [the angelic governor-general of
> the Magnetic City], for me he is an athletic, perfectly
> ignorant, entirely unphilosophical young man. He is
> a big baby, who does not know the ABC of life. . . .
> Our everyday world is full of such cases as the angel.
> The cowboy, the aristocrat, the great athlete, the ace
> airman; each in his way is a perfect being, but com-
> pletely stupid. For instance, the aristocrat means the
> average, unreal gentleman with faultless and beauti-
> ful manners, bred to be noble and beautiful like the
> swan. A Bolingbroke or a Chesterfield is exceedingly
> intelligent: they are able to *see through* themselves and
> so are no longer perfections. . . . Anyone in whom
> you detect *consciousness of self*—capable of objective
> understanding of himself—shrinks in your estima-
> tion . . . Now to be a real angel, and, just on the
> same principle, to be God, you must be entirely

stupid. We are compelled deeply to admire such
perfections. And it is in no way to take away from
the splendid pre-eminence of God—in no way to
diminish one's awe of his might—if one said one did
not desire to *be* God, or to be an angel.

(MG, 139)

This pejorative theology will seem less paradoxical when
we realize that Lewis' afterlife is not a spiritual but a material one, and that the primacy of "God" has nothing to do
with the usual perfections or entelechies but is a matter of
sheer overwhelming power.

For the moment, we must understand how this new
signifying axis—Weakness/Intelligence vs. vitalistic, mindless Strength—reverses and restructures the polarities of
the older model. The Tarr figure—potential Shavian
superman and pure eye—now occupies the place of
Pullman, the empty or abstract subject, the intellectual
without any form of effective power. The Kreisler figure,
meanwhile, disperses altogether: as the place of sheer instinct, it can in no way be identified with the new term of
angelic strength, which is predicated, as we shall see
shortly, on the very absence of instincts, and most
specifically of the sexual one, constituting on the contrary
the embodiment of a strange and nonhuman indifference.
Kreisler's twin functions are in fact in the new system radically differentiated: and the instinctual component now
presumably the negative of angelic indifference—becomes
structurally and explicitly disjoined from his other role as
the pariah or victim.

It remains to find a place for the two other terms which
have emerged in the course of this discussion: the mindless
peons and the malignant potency and conspiratorial intent
of the Bailiff, which may now be seen as the subcontraries of human intelligence and angelic indifference respectively. A system thus emerges which can be laid out in the
following way:

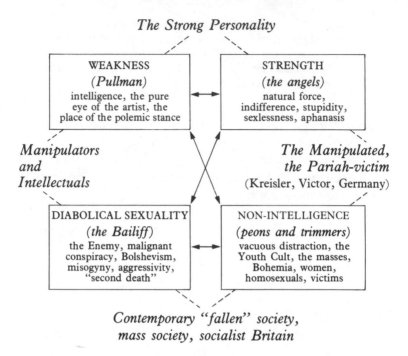

The Strong Personality

| WEAKNESS
(*Pullman*)
intelligence, the pure
eye of the artist, the
place of the polemic stance | STRENGTH
(*the angels*)
natural force,
indifference, stupidity,
sexlessness, aphanasis |

Manipulators   *The Manipulated,*
and   *the Pariah-victim*
Intellectuals   (Kreisler, Victor, Germany)

| DIABOLICAL SEXUALITY
(*the Bailiff*)
the Enemy, malignant
conspiracy, Bolshevism,
misogyny, aggressivity,
"second death" | NON-INTELLIGENCE
(*peons and trimmers*)
vacuous distraction, the
Youth Cult, the masses,
Bohemia, women,
homosexuals, victims |

Contemporary "fallen" society,
mass society, socialist Britain

On this reading, the "ideal" of the strong leader or "strong" personality in Lewis remains precisely that—a dead letter, a contradiction in terms, an ideal and impossible synthesis of incompatible characteristics, a merely logical possibility which no narrative—let alone real history itself—can concretely generate. Lewis' narratives know this, whether he does or not: Hitler is for example in his eponymous book[5] by no means evoked as the superman of conventional Nazi propaganda, but rather as an average and quintessentially representative German type: this was itself no doubt part of Hitler's rhetorical staging of himself, yet the attitude compares favorably with Pound's manifestly hero-worshipping celebrations of Mussolini. Indeed, the German "position" (Kreisler in retrospect, the Victor of *The Revenge for Love* in a metaphorical sense) is here that of the maimed victim or pariah: someone who

5. See Appendix.

unites natural strength with a fundamental lack of intelligence that makes him ripe for exploitation and manipula-
tion by the demonic forces of the Bailiff (or of Bolshevism).

Nor is artistic genius any longer a full or positive term
either, but rather a privative position in which the debility
of the pure eye or observing ego is not, as in *Tarr*, rationalized into a value in its own right, but rather openly ac-
knowledged. Still, it is from the standpoint of this position
of combined weakness and intelligence that Lewis' own
great polemics against the modern age are launched. It will
now therefore be useful to make a brief detour through
them, in order to observe the ways in which the ideological
contradictions of this narrative system are inscribed in
what presents itself as purely conceptual discourse.

7/
THE JAUNDICED EYE

As to what this formally fixed 'self' is, and how to
describe it, I have plainly indicated how I would go
about that. From the outset I gave away the principle of
my activity, and made no disguise of its partisan, even
its specialist character. So my philosophic position could
almost be called an occupational one, except that my
occupation is not one that I have received by accident or
mechanically inherited, but is one that I chose as
responding to an exceptional instinct or bias. . . . With
as much definiteness as that, whatever I, for my part,
say, can be traced back to an organ; but in my case it is
the *eye*. It is in the service of the things of vision that my
ideas are mobilized.

Time and Western Man

 HE DISCOURSE OF *TARR* WAS PRESOCIAL
or prepolitical in the way in which its
constellation of national types lacked a
formal ground: Paris, the "real" Paris,
a place of "sacrifice" (that is, of the prodigious heroism and agony of France in
the trenches), is effectively bracketed from the outset by
the first two sentences of the novel. This suspension of the
social ground is to be sure what allows *Tarr's* free-floating
character system to be projected out as an allegorical cosmos; yet its absence is implicit in the system itself, which
makes no place for characterizations of or generalizations
about the social.

With the new libidinal apparatus, this also changes, as
we have seen; and the "break" is followed, not only by
narratives of a wholly new order, but also by a sudden
release of impressive quantities of what must be called cultural criticism. The Lewis of the twenties and thirties thus

launches himself into a tireless polemic production, of which the principal monuments are *The Art of Being Ruled* (1925), *The Lion and the Fox* (1926), *Time and Western Man* (1927), and *Men Without Art* (1934) (not to speak of journalism like *Hitler* [1931]): politics, political theory, metaphysics, aesthetics—such is the variety of registers on which a single theme—the loss of reality in modern life, or, if you prefer a somewhat franker version, the systematic undermining of the European White Male Will,[1] is implacably pursued. Lewis' view of politics as "the struggle for power"[2]—so fundamental that, as we have already seen, it extends even to the afterlife and the dynamics of Heaven—determines a Nietzschean analysis in which the sapping and subversion of "Strength" is implicitly attributed to malign agency (Lewis' villains are all in this sense Nietzschean priests, intellectuals driven by *ressentiment*) and explicitly identified in the various forms of class war (Marxism), sex war (feminism), and the strategic valorization of the immature (the Youth Cult) and of the "third sex."

The central philosophical exhibit in this wide-ranging cultural analysis is however the attack on the Time Cult in an immense and prophetic book (*Time and Western Man*), published in the same year as Heidegger's *Sein und Zeit*, which might, indeed, have furnished its principal exhibit. The central thesis, that contemporary consciousness, from Bergson to Whitehead and on, but also modern art, and the modern sensibility in all its manifestations, are saturated by an original and historically new sense of temporality, has become a commonplace of modernist criticism. Today, when the phenomenological celebration of temporality seems a thing of the past—the constitutive feature of a now classical modernism, rather than of a language-centered postmodernism—Lewis' hostile anatomy of the

---

1. See Wyndham Lewis, *Hitler* (London: Chatto & Windus, 1931), pp. 119–124.

2. Wyndham Lewis, *Rude Assignment* (London: Hutchinson, 1950), p. 162.

time-impulse is perhaps a salutary corrective and is drawn on a scale which sweeps virtually everything in the then contemporary culture—from Joyce and Pound, to Spengler, William James, Watsonian Behavioralism—into its net.

Here too, Lewis' text may be read as an unexpected working out and documentation of the Nietzschean "Uses and Abuses of History," in a quite different cultural context. On his diagnosis, the commitment to temporality as an experience, the valorization of historicity and *durée* over the timeless objectivity of the lived present, stands at the very center of the unreality of twentieth century man (sic), dissolving his experience, reducing his ego or psychic unity to a bundle of disparate moments, discrediting abstraction in the name of sheer physiological and phenomenal sensation, and in the process giving rise to the compensatory mechanisms of all the false gods, nationalisms, and collective hysterias, through which the individual vainly attempts to repossess a measure of substantiality.

Not the content of this elaborate onslaught—as a neutral description of the originality of modern consciousness it is surely unexceptionable—but rather its form is fundamentally problematic. The theme of time is here an instrument of analysis and descriptive explanation which is then called upon to function as a causal hypothesis. It is perfectly appropriate to adopt a thematic lens through which to register the (otherwise imperceptible) emergence of a new *Weltanschauung:* Ortega's indictment of "mass man," Adorno and Horkheimer's analysis of "instrumental thinking," MacLuhan's account of print-culture and electronic culture, Deleuze and Guattari's unmasking of familialism and psychologistic reduction, Barthes' isolation of the category of "naturality," the Althusserian repudiation of "humanism" (individualism), offer a wide range of such themes, which all in one way or another aim at "estranging" the present such that we can get some handle on the way in which we are programmed by its ideological tendencies and epistemic categories.

Such diagnoses, however, tend fatally to reorganize themselves into "theories of history"[3]: that is, to become mesmerized by their own representational framework in such a way that they misread the organizational device by which they were able to narrate historical change for the objective force or cause responsible for the change in question. The cultural symptom is now denounced as its own self-fulfilling and self-perpetuating executor: and the "belief" in temporality effectively transforms our experience of time and space itself and infects the underlying reality of which it was supposed to be a misrepresentation. At that point, however, the ideology has presumably become true: and the phenomenology of temporality henceforth offers a correct and perfectly adequate analysis of experience thus corrupted and restructured by the Time Cult. Under these circumstances, it is the diagnostician who is put on the defensive, and of whom it must be asked in the name of what and from what Archimedean point he is able to "reject" the object of his critique, now no longer a mere ideological fad, but rather a social and existential reality. This new dilemma then tends to generate a second-level and compensatory vision of history, in which a degraded present is judged and repudiated in terms of this or that image of a valorized past.

We already know Lewis' uniquely disarming "solution" to this problem, which marks a certain advance over such nostalgic historiography. He willingly admits the ideological thrust of his own critique: no placeless historicism, it is openly identified as the defense of a certain praxis and the polemic projection of a concrete embattled situation. Yet that praxis and that situation are themselves defined in purely individual and well-nigh nominalist

3. See for a further discussion of such "theories of history," my *Marxism and Form* (Princeton: Princeton University Press, 1971), pp. 319–326.

terms: "whatever I, for my part, say, can be traced back to
. . . the *eye*"; "my philosophic position could. . . . be
called an occupational one" (*TWM*, 138, 137). An absolute
critique of culture finds itself grounded in the thoroughly
relativized position of the painter, whose own vested interest lies in the desperate establishment of a more propitious
ideological and cultural space in which to do his own
work. Yet it cannot be said that he managed to keep faith
with this uncomfortably honest and precarious stance. The
anomalous situation of the painter finds itself slowly absolutized against its will and imperceptibly turns back into
an affirmation of intellectual life in general ("intelligence")
and artistic creation in particular. So an idiosyncratic and
individualistic posture at length becomes indistinguishable
from the most banal defenses of (Western) culture—or in
more concrete terms, the privileges of Western intellectuals—against incipient barbarism. Such reversals are, as
we shall see in a moment, the consequences of an insuffi-
ciently reflexive position, of the failure of Lewis' situational self-consciousness to become genuinely dialectical.

For the moment, it is of more interest to observe the
conceptual paradoxes which result from the idealist framework[4] in which the culture critique itself is conceived:

> In *Time and Western Man* Lewis had argued against
> the behaviorists, who, he said, insulted the human
> race by reducing people to a set of mechanical ges-
> tures. In his fiction of this period, Lewis employed
> the same reductionism, originally for satiric pur-
> poses. But the satire turned back on itself as Lewis

---

4. Idealist in the strict sense, of positing ideas as the ultimate cause of historical events: Lewis' account of his procedures in *Time and Western Man* is most
revealing in this regard: "Suppose that you advance such a statement as the
following. '(1) Sacco and Vanzetti are executed under such and such circumstances. (2) That is owing to the over-emotional strain in the composition of
Hegel, that made his mind an imperfect philosophical instrument. (3) The reason
that that philosophical instrument exercised the influence it did was on account
of the romanticism prevalent in the years succeeding the French Revolution. (4)
Because it served the ends of this person and that,' etc., etc." (p. ix)

came increasingly to believe that human beings in
fact amounted to no more than the behaviorists said:
a complex system of predictable twitches. What
began as satirical strategy ended up convincing the
strategist, as though Swift had turned cannibal.[5]

So the phenomenologists of time are transformed, by their
own ideas, into the insubstantial hollow creatures of the
time flats; in *The Writer and the Absolute* (1952), Lewis
writes a tract against political *engagement* which is itself a
political pamphlet; while in *The Human Age*, the
humanism of the Bailiff and the Devil is denounced as
what ultimately vilifies human life and empties it of its
dignity, even though God—presumably an antihumanist
and a proponent of Absolutes—turns out to "value man."

Yet the most striking version of this antinomy remains
the discrepancy between the theory and the practice of
Time and Western Man. This work decisively repudiates
theories of history as such, and lucidly identifies them as
cults of the *Zeitgeist*, and modish rationalizations of the
present itself, dishonest celebrations of a fetishized and
fetishizing time-sensibility. All such theories, he tells us,
are

> presided over by a time-keeping, chronologically-
> real, super-historic, Mind, like some immense
> stunt-figure symbolizing Fashion, ecstatically assur-
> ing its customers that although fashions are periodic,
> as they must and indeed ought to be, nevertheless, by
> some mysterious rule, each one is *better* than the last,
> and should (so the advertisement would run) be paid
> *more* for than the last, in money or in blood.
>
> (*TWM*, 218)

Yet Lewis' is *also* a theory of history; and to characterize
the modern mind in terms of its cult of the *Zeitgeist* is
surely thereby at one and the same time to denounce this
particular *Zeitgeist* by means of the very conceptual

---

5. Robert C. Elliott, *The Power of Satire* (Princeton: Princeton University
Press, 1968), pp. 236–237.

categories which were to have been discredited in the first place.

Such antinomies are of course not peculiarly Lewis', but are ultimately attributable to cultural criticism itself as a form. It is clear that Lewis' polemic pamphlets must be replaced within a whole corpus of such productions in the interwar period, which constitutes a veritable discursive genre—what we will call the "culture critique"—and numbers such influential texts as Ortega's *Rebelión de las masas*, Benda's *Trahison des clercs*, Scheler's call to cultural regeneration, Heidegger's stigmatization of the inauthenticity of the anonymous and depersonalized subject of the modern industrial city, not excluding the more "positive" appeals to authority of a Babbitt or a Charles Maurras, whose ideas, along with many of those previously mentioned, found a congenial forum in T. S. Eliot's revue *The Criterion* throughout this period. Not that any of these positions can lay claim to intellectual originality: in the main, they tend to exploit, with varying degrees of ingenuity, counterrevolutionary theories and arguments developed generations earlier by Taine and Nietzsche (when not by Edmund Burke himself). Yet in the mechanized city of the interwar period, such concepts find a rich new field of manoeuvre and a far wider social and ideological resonance.

What they can now express is that apocalyptic vision of the end of Western civilization to which Spengler gave representation, and which is eloquently dramatized by Valéry's cry: "Nous autres civilizations, nous savons maintenant que nous sommes mortels!" Yet as we have already seen, the exhilarating pathos of this decline of civilization conceals the more prosaic realities of the crisis of a class, and of the disastrous inflation that marginalized whole strata of *rentiers* and middle and lower middle class savings-book holders. Such a dreary experience of inexorable financial strangulation has about it little enough of the Wagnerian intoxication of a Spengler. Yet inflation is preeminently the hard school in which the middle classes, from Balzac to Lewis himself, and beyond them, to the Americans of the 1970s, learn that History exists; and the dizzying perspective of proletarianization which it opened up after World War I was to drive two European petty bourgeoisies into the security of institutional fascism.

The intellectual authority of the culture critique depends on the repression of this concrete social situation, and on the projection of its anxieties into some more timeless realm of moral judgement: the sense of placelessness, the illusion of absolute values thereby produced, discloses the constitutive idealism of this genre, which formally tends to express a classical conservatism even where its content seems to contradict the form. Lewis was often, in this sense, merely a conservative. Where his polemics become formally and ideologically revealing are those moments·in which the idealistic framework of the culture critique is briefly and with fitful, energetic impatience unmasked. At such moments, indeed, the rhetoric of conservative thought, which has ended up believing in its own official solicitude for Culture, gives way to the unpleasant and embarrassing cynicism of protofascism itself, which knows its intellectual practice as something other than the disinterested guardianship of universal values. In these moments, an embattled and Darwinian defense of the subject's own threatened position and individual vested interests breaks through the universalizing pretence of philosophical discourse; and the rights of privilege are openly affirmed against the threat to the self of some genuinely universal vision of human society. This is, it seems to me, the essential spirit of Lewis' otherwise conceptually untenable "justification by the eye" of his "occupational" philosophy: the return of the concrete individual situation effectively demystifies the culture critique as a form along with the classic conservative rhetoric associated with it. Meanwhile the protofascist gesture has the virtue of all polarization in the way in which, unavoidably, if only for a brief moment, it causes the ultimate political options to rise before us.

Left/liberal culture critiques are no less problematic than the conservative ones here under discussion: for they also perpetuate the idealism of this framework and suggest that cultural change and social renovation can be achieved by changes in thinking, or elevations in the level of consciousness. Charles Reich's symptomatic *Greening of America* offers a particularly coarse and revealing example of this strategy, which affirms the spiritual power of the counterculture to transform American capitalism, thereby rendering political activity unnecessary. In works like these, the more general antipolitical ideology of liberal reformism is reduplicated and reinforced by the more specific professional or "occupational" ideology of intellectuals, who have an objective and constitutional vested interest in the autonomy of ideas and cultural phenomena: it is an interest which finds privileged expression in the addiction to the *examen de conscience,* in a belief in the primacy of theory over practice and in the immediate practical consequences of just such purely theoretical rectifications and "revolutions" in consciousness.

We must however note a significant difference between these liberal or left-oriented critiques of culture and the conservative ones mentioned earlier, including those of Lewis himself. Liberal or left-oriented idealism, from Godwin and Schiller to Charles Reich, aims essentially at the transformation of the *self,* at some fundamental transformation of our own consciousness (which will then make an external revolution in the institutions unnecessary): the culture critique of the Right, however, takes as the basic object of its diagnosis the consciousness of *other people.* Its working categories are therefore inevitably those of otherness and engage a peculiar dialectic of mirror images which does not in the end leave the place of the judging subject unscathed. Nietzsche's concept of *ressentiment* is perhaps the archetypal embodiment of such a dialectic: *ressentiment* marks the Other as reactive and attributes the vengeance taken by the weak over the strong to the former's envy. The diagnosis is then extrapolated to social revolution itself (which was perhaps always its secret object of meditation) and explains the latter in terms of the *ressentiment* of the have-nots for the haves. Yet in a world dominated by the weak and their various slave-ethics, Nietzsche's own position must necessarily be reactive; indeed, the bitterness with which the "phenomenon" of *ressentiment* is inevitably evoked—and it is the fundamental conceptual category of all late-nineteenth and early twentieth century counterrevolutionary literature[6]—suggests that, as an explanatory category, *ressentiment* is always itself the product of *ressentiment*.

Meanwhile, if the Other is thus conceived, *en masse*, to be an inert, purely reactive collectivity, passively worked over by its own compulsions, the need for a second-degree account of *ressentiment* arises. The difficulty is perhaps a narrative one: an object which is conceived in terms of sheer otherness cannot by definition become an agent in its own right, for then the Nietzschean slaves would find themselves displaced into the category of the Strong, their reaction thereby transformed into a form of genuine action and autonomous self-generating energy. The apparent actions of this anonymous collective Other thus demand completion by the hypothesis of an agent responsible for them in its turn, in whom the dialectic of *ressentiment* is recapitulated on a higher level. And since the culture critique has been conceived as the diagnosis of pernicious attitudes and toxic ideas, the agents of cultural decay are specified in advance and can be no other than the very guardians of culture, the intellectuals themselves, by definition disgruntled and embittered, failed artists and

6. See my Gissing and Conrad chapters in the forthcoming *The Political Unconscious* (Ithaca, N.Y.: Cornell University Press).

would-be unsuccessful politicians—in short, the very archetype of *ressentiment* at its purest.

So at the term of all culture critiques it is the intellectual who emerges as the scapegoat-enemy, whether in the guise of Benda's "cleric," of Nietzsche's ascetic priest, of Lewis' Bloomsbury set and his millionaire Bolsheviks, or indeed that cosmopolitan intelligentsia of all the European countries, veritable Jews of the spirit if not of the flesh, of whom Goebbels is said to have remarked that when he saw one, he drew his revolver. Yet this climactic identification of the intellectual as the fountainhead of cultural and social corruption is a "theory" itself devised by intellectuals.

This is the spirit in which Lewis and his historian-hero (in *Self Condemned*) attribute to Marxism the ultimate responsibility for the decline of the West:

> It is [René Harding's] view that the liberal idealism
> of the nineteenth century would, left to itself, have
> eventuated in a twentieth century rebirth, wonder-
> fully assisted by the burst of inventive genius coincid-
> ing with the liberal climax in the second decade of
> this century [Lloyd George's Health Insurance Act is
> meant]—that so supported, this idealism could have
> produced a new age of social justice, had it not been
> for the intervention of the Marxist ideology [with its]
> incitement to hatred and civil war [and its] doctrine
> of the necessity of catastrophe. (*SC*, 91)

Such a view may usefully be juxtaposed with that of historical materialism itself, for which theories (not excluding Marxism itself), ideologies, opinions and attitudes, and even cultural practices of the type denounced by Lewis in his various attacks on what was later to become the "counter-culture," are neither historical forces in their own right nor mere reflexes of economic or infrastructural developments; but must be seen as components and integral parts of a more complex and concrete social process.

Such a process can be "modelled" and formulated in

various ways: the one which has evidently been central here is the conception of reification, which, as Lukács elaborated it, links Marx's analysis of commodity fetishism with the Weberian concept of rationalization (both of them drawing in different ways on the classical diagnosis of fragmentation and of the psychic "division of labor" so central in German idealism).[7] Reification designates a structure which is at one and the same time a process, so that it enforces a genuinely historical perspective from the outset.

Meanwhile, the concept is a mediatory one, which describes an infrastructural dynamic—the new social rhythms introduced by factory production, the market system, a generalized money economy, the commodification of labor power, and the omnipresence of the commodity form as such—in terms which can immediately be reappropriated for the formal analysis of cultural and ideological phenomena as well. The mediatory capacity of such a "code" or terminological system thus allows us to cut through the false problems of a more mechanical Marxism on the one hand (in particular, that of the uneven relationship between base and superstructure), while on the other it precludes the artificial isolation of culture and thought in some closed and autonomous realm of their own, as tends to be the case even in the best histories of ideas or of artistic forms.

From this perspective, then, contemporary time philosophies, and the new lived experience of temporality which they express, are to be grasped as features of a more universal process of fragmentation. Time, now semiautonomized, is dissociated into the two incommensurable

7. The fundamental text is of course "Reification and the Consciousness of the Proletariat," in Georg Lukács, *History and Class Consciousness*, translated by Rodney Livingstone (Cambridge: MIT Press, 1971), pp. 83–222. And see for a fuller discussion of the uses of this concept in literary interpretation, my forthcoming *Political Unconscious*.

realms of the quantified and instrumentalized clock time of the world of work,[8] and the henceforth marginalized "lived" time of what has now become private or subjective experience.

But if this is the case, then Bergson's description of these two forms of temporality cannot be said to be *wrong:* on the contrary, it constitutes a phenomenological description of the life experience of subjects under late capitalism which gives us useful thematic material for the reconstruction of this experience in the form of a historical situation, a life dilemma, a determinate contradiction. What Lewis' implacable critique reveals is that Bergsonianism is also an *ideology:* that is, that to the dilemma it so usefully describes and thematizes it also proposes a privatizing response, in its valorization and mystique of an authentic, personal temporality to be cultivated in opposition to the inauthentic time of factory space. A social contradiction which on its own terms could only project a political and a revolutionary resolution is thereby transformed and "reduced" to a matter of individual—moral, psychological, or aesthetic—choice: thus conceived, the "problem" becomes its own solution. Bergson's thought remains locked in an essentially idealistic framework in which the dissociation of time can only be seen (and dealt with) in terms of spiritual or "existential" experience.

Lewis' keen sense of the ideological function of time philosophies in general and Bergson in particular can now be explained: their conceptual dilemmas are a mirror image of his own and are reproduced by the no less contradictory but provocative and perverse reversal of their

8. E. P. Thompson, "Time, Work Discipline, and Industrial Capitalism," *Past and Present*, No. 38, (December, 1967), pp. 56–97. The analysis of the "instrumentalization" of modern consciousness is one of the fundamental achievements of the Frankfurt School: see, for example, T. W. Adorno and Max Horkheimer, *Dialectic of Enlightenment*, translated by John Cumming (New York: Herder and Herder, 1972), and Marx Horkheimer, *Eclipse of Reason* (New York: Seabury, 1974).

own positions by *Time and Western Man:* thus what Bergson valorizes—the existential experience of inner, lived time—Lewis repudiates. Yet for both this essentially symptomatic experience is the result, not of structural modifications in social life, but rather of the very *concepts* that seek to describe and define it. Bergson's philosophical distinction between the two forms of time will presumably allow his readers to identify the more authentic zone of temporal experience for the purposes of reorganizing their individual lives around their deepening perception of it; while, for Lewis, far more resolutely social, the valorized concept will itself generate a fatal temporalization of social life in general.

Lewis indeed told us repeatedly that he meant to remain on the surface of things: the result is that his dramatic account of ideological production, unable to be grounded and completed by a vision of the total social process of which ideology is a part, finds itself deflected into conspiracy theory. Meanwhile, thus effectively bracketted and reduced to its own surface by these procedures, "reality" takes its revenge and henceforth offers nothing but the shifting shapes and sheer exteriority of the raw materials of satiric production to the hypertrophied ego of the cultural critic, who, seeking to grapple with these surfaces, now is himself implacably transformed into the pure painterly eye of the satirist-enemy.

8/
THE SEX OF ANGELS

'How is it that no one ever sees *himself* in the public
mirror—in official Fiction? That is the essential point of
my argument with Li. Everybody gazes into the public
mirror. No one sees himself! What is the use of a mirror
then if it reflects a World, always, without the principal
person—the Me?'

The Apes of God

ATIRE WAS NOT, IN LEWIS' MATURE
aesthetic, one mode of discourse among
others, but rather the very essence of art
itself, vorticism or expressionism riding
in the Trojan Horse of a generic designation, a style which is now in reality a
whole world-view.[1] The concept of satire generalizes Tarr's
view of art: "the armoured hide of the hippopotamus, the
shell of the tortoise, feathers and machinery" become extended into the very fabric of the universe, which no longer
has a place for the "naked pulsing and moving of the soft
inside of life." Thus absolutized, satire recovers something
of its primitive power and its most archaic vocation: it is
no longer a choice or stylistic option within the world, but
the latter's overriding law and inner dynamic. Laughter
and aggressivity are thereby no longer functions of the

1. See Note 10, Chapter Two.

individual subject, but rather terrifying and impersonal forces which sweep the surfaces of a two-dimensional planet.

As Robert C. Elliott shows in *The Power of Satire*, the literary mode has its prehistoric origins in the magical curse and the ritual expulsion of the scapegoat. Satire is thus from its beginnings the negative expression of the sacred, which as *mana* and *taboo* is life-giving and deadly all at once, its destructive purification serving as the complement to the phallic celebration of fertility rites.

The earliest "satirists" are therefore powerful magicians, whose word literally kills in the shame cultures in which it is ritually wielded: in this social context, "satiric" activity is institutionalized and requires no independent justification. In the polis, however, as both tragedy and satire become secularized and disengaged from their ritual origins, their practice comes to demand theoretical legitimation, and a social functionality is evoked of which, in the case of tragedy, Aristotle's *Poetics* is the most systematic description. The case for a cathartic function of satire, however, requires a historical rather than a psychological framework: the ritual cleansing of the polis necessarily implies a moral degeneration of society from those older virtues of a simpler and healthier community to which the satirist, from Aristophanes and Juvenal to the Old Testament prophets, demands a return. The great satirists have thus been predominantly conservative, and their golden ages ideological fictions.

The ethical justification of vernacular satire ("the castigation of vice") would seem to be a mere formalization of this now sedimented regressive social vision. At any rate, Elliott's work suggests that the archaic impulse of satire was rigorously nonmoral, and Lewis will himself repeatedly emphasize the ritualistic and violent features of a mode of language he felt himself to have virtually reinvented. Yet this reemergence of the archaic, and the weakening of the social or ethical justification of the mode—a tendency in all powerful satire (think only of the ambiguity of this impulse in Swift!)—now generates a new formal dilemma which returns upon satiric practice to problematize it in an unexpected way. In the name of what, indeed, can the satirist now take it upon himself to speak for the collectivity—to castigate, for the sake of some imaginary community, follies and vices which are themselves profoundly social in nature? In this situation, the content of satire slowly becomes transformed: continuing all the while to denounce his traditional objects, the satirist becomes self-conscious about his own activity. With the problematization of his own place as a judging and observing subject, he begins to reckon himself into the universal condemnation which only awaited his own presence to be complete. At length, in *Timon of Athens* or *Le Misanthrope*, bile and misanthropy come to be numbered among the vices to be castigated, and satire squares its own circle with a portrait of what Elliott has called "the satirist satirized." With this, however, a dialectically new form is generated, driven by an internal contradiction that has left such works among the permanent enigmas of literary history.

Lewis himself produced a striking example of this curious form in his late autobiographical novel, *Self Condemned*, surely the most desolate of all his works, in which the history professor, René Harding, exiled by choice from what he considers to be the establishment radicalism of British university life, enters the glacial void of provincial Canada and knows, at the end, a virtual living death. The ambiguity of this fate is essentially a structural one: it is never altogether clear what in this combative and opinionated work is in the long run being censured. Harding is no doubt a casualty and a victim, first of the British power structure, then of the accidents of war, the dreariness of colonial life, the hostility and eventual suicide of his own wife. Yet at the same time he is just as clearly a snob and a prig, an authoritarian husband, the very epitome of emotional repression, and a malicious ironist and misanthrope, who, as the title suggests, bears full responsibility for everything that happens to him. Yet as we have already noted in an earlier context, there is about this interpretive ambiguity none of the stable moral irony of a Henry James, or of Ford's *The Good Soldier*. The effect of *Self Condemned* is a good deal more forbidding and alienating than the most thoroughgoing ethical reevaluation and condemnation of an earlier self. The narrative "voice" in *Self Condemned* alternates between the pathos of a total identification with the hero and the icy objectivity of the most hostile and impersonal judgement; between an instinctive self-defense of the ego and an almost pathologically depersonalized inspection of it from without, as though it belonged to someone else.

This variation in narrative distance, which excludes any compromise unity of point of view between the existential experience of the subject and the possibility of moral judgements on it, is determined by an instinctual interpretation of the forces at work in Harding's ruin. For Lewis, what is at stake in the process is the very fate of the negative, the critical, the "satiric" itself:

> The process of radical revaluation, the process which was responsible for the revolutionary character of his work, that analysis, turned inwards (upon, for instance, such things as the intimate structure of domestic life), this furious analysis began disintegrating many relationships and attitudes which only an exceptionally creative spirit, under very favourable conditions, can afford to dispense with. (*SC*, 401)

Such a passage suggests that for Lewis the satiric impulse is very far from being a mere formal or discursive option. It is no neutral system of representation, but rather a dangerous force, that cannot be wielded with impunity, that threatens, in situations like that of Harding, to return destructively upon the satirist himself, searing everything it finds there and leaving "a glacial shell of a man" behind it. The repression of emotion must then be read as a defense mechanism, the attempt to master this terrible force and contain it beneath the civilizing conventions of the superego. Characteristically, the final "locking up" of Harding's personality in ultimate depersonalization and spiritual death follows immediately upon a violent outburst of rage and hostility against his best friend. Harding's fate is indeed a kind of preventive suicide, a way of neutralizing, by self-imposed emotional isolation, the deadly instinctual force of which he is the bearer.

Self Condemned suggests that the question of the magic or archaic origins of satire must now be reviewed in a new light. It is often suggested that contemporary life—far from being completely rationalized—is riddled with prelogical and superstitious thought modes which are so many survivals of older types of social behavior. If so, such patterns should not be taken as evidence for an archetypal collective consciousness, but rather as evidence for the way in which, even in the most advanced mode of production, there is a layered sedimentation and persistence of types of alienation specific to more archaic modes: thus, the commodity reification of capitalism does not supersede, but is rather laid over and coexists with the power systems of precapitalist societies—as, for instance, in *machismo* and sexism—as well as the most archaic division of labor of tribal society itself, in the form of the inequality between men and women and between youth and elder.

Yet the prelogical force of all the fears associated with the magical curse and the satiric onslaught is perhaps better understood in terms of the aggressor than of his targets. Not the victim, but rather the satirist himelf still obscurely believes in the annihilating force of his incantation. He is indeed the only one in an adequate position to measure the whole range and potency of the destructive impulses he bears within himself; he alone recoils before the insatiable and unmotivated force of the aggressivity of which he is the vehicle. The satirist is in this sense his own first victim; and his misanthropy is accompanied with an ineradicable sense of guilt no less intense for all the purely symbolic or imaginary nature of his gesture. There would in fact seem to be substantial clinical documentation for the notion that the unprepared eruption of aggressive fantasies and impulses can paralyze the psyche and plunge it into a deeper and more pathological despondency than the acting out of aggressivity itself, whose violent expression necessarily brings some relief. In this sense, however, the aesthetic distance of satire as a purely symbolic act must leave such impulses intact and relatively unsatisfied.

We have already shown how the narrative model of *Tarr* effectively recontains such destructive impulses, which are with Kreisler the object of representation within a closed system. The pseudocouple is in this respect a kind of holding operation, in which impulses are at one and the same time rigidly checked, and yet exasperated by an oscillating movement in which they find no satisfactory symbolic outlet. The new libidinal apparatus of the transindividual forces of the great ideologies, the forces of cultural corruption, the Time Cult, the corrupt intelligentsia, the essentially collective dynamics of feminism or homosexual militancy, now makes for a grid in which psychic forces can know analogous figuration and are freed to capture and to expropriate narrative systems of which they were hitherto merely the bound components.

Alongside a psychoanalytic investigation of the rich biographical symptoms in Lewis' work, there is room for a structural description of their textual functioning, a description which has an intelligibility of its own, quite different from that of diagnosis or causal hypothesis. It is clear, for example, that Lewis' misogyny may quite appropriately be read as the pathological symptom of some deeper character disorder in the man himself. Yet it can also be read as a figural pretext for the immanent play of aggressivity within the text itself. On this view, even aggressivity would not be read as a secondary phenomenon that needed some further, primary explanation (as in hypotheses about sadomasochism, the aggressive instinct, the authoritarian personality and the like) but is grasped as the expression in instinctual terms of the purely formal movement and consequences of satire as a symbolic act.

In this light, the later works can be seen to form a kind of instinctual *combinatoire* or permutation system, projecting all the logically possible variations on the basic structure of the aggressive assault implicit in satire. The narratives then register the systematic modifications in the way in which victim and aggressor are conceived and are formally determined by the distinct kinds of psychic satisfactions available in these various structural combinations. Thus the almost exclusively homosexual world of *The Apes of God* offers a field in which the satiric impulse may with impunity be given full rein. Insofar as the characters are identified with women, they are marked out as victims and satiric objects of the first magnitude; while the fact that they are biological males releases the satirist-aggressor from his usual guilt feelings. Thus a veritable holocaust can be celebrated; yet paradoxically, save for a halfhearted fist fight at the end, little overt physical violence is registered in the narrative. The satiric impulse has found a purely symbolic vehicle in which to inscribe its figures and invest its dynamism and does not require the ultimately self-destructive symbolic representation of "real" death.

In *Self Condemned,* on the other hand, this impulse, driven underground by the conventions of narrative realism just as much as by the psychic repression of its hero, knows something like a "return of the repressed," which oddly punctuates the narrative line with gratuitous violence, mostly in the form of the unnatural deaths of a series of women figures. Harding leaves England and his mother dies: this is perhaps the primal event that founds the series. Then the cleaning lady, Mrs. Harradson, falls down the cellar steps and breaks her neck: utterly unmotivated by the plot, such an episode cannot but suggest a deeper level of intelligibility which the official content of the text means to withhold from us. Equally shocking and insistent, equally unmotivated, is the following glimpse of a minor accident to Harding's sister, as she belatedly leaves the boat train which is to carry him into exile:

> He entered a carriage and sprang to an open window, where he was just in time to see her jump from the moving train and fall on the platform. The human body is not a square object like a trunk, and when it falls it tends to roll. In her case it rolled towards the train. But a porter seized her shoulders and stopped the roll. In doing this, he apparently lost his balance and went down backwards with his legs in the air. In the same instant Helen, now no longer a rolling body, but in command of her limbs once more, sprang to her feet, and René momentarily had the impression that it was she who was knocking over the railway porter. (*SC*, 139)

Not only does Harding's projective mechanism convert this rescue into a kind of assault; on a more formal and impersonal level, the accident itself can be read as the attempt of the satiric impulse itself to convert its most recalcitrant organic object, the human body, into the more propitious material of sheer externality and inertia.

Meanwhile, in the Canadian subplot of the work, the likeable Mrs. McAffie, whose body is found in the ashes of the great hotel fire, proves in reality to have been bludgeoned to death. This episode allows us to observe the multiple investment of Lewis' libidinal apparatus, and in particular its overdetermination by political as well as psychic impulses. For Affie—on one level simply another in the series of women-victims we have been enumerating—is also characterized as a "decaying gentlewoman," who on a quite different level of representation thus stands as an allegorical representation of social strata pauperized by inflation. Her murderer, Martin, turns out to have been the secret owner of the social microcosm of the hotel itself: with his characteristic manners, a caricature of the stuffiest

British "respectability," Martin thus reenacts for Lewis (and for Harding) the betrayal and abdication of a corrupt Tory ruling class.

Yet on the instinctual level he is simply a double or alter ego of Harding himself. The Martin figure therefore provides for a kind of Freudian "splitting" of Harding's fundamental (and ambiguous) "semes." The instinctual "seme" identifies the two figures as doubles of one another, thereby revealing the negative "truth" of the main plot: Martin-Harding as the aggressor and murderer of women victims. Meanwhile the political "seme" functions to reseparate and distance these two figures from one another: Martin must now, on this level, be taken as Harding's opposite, as the embodiment of the corrupt establishment against which Harding is himself in revolt, and for whose aggressive crimes he can therefore (from this new perspective) no longer be held responsible. The "molar" or political level thus serves to recontain the brief instinctual revelation, and to overdetermine and rationalize it back out of existence by means of conspiracy theory.

Yet such containment is fitful and unstable at best. At length, the aggressive impulse demands fulfillment; and in the climactic moment of the work, Harding's wife, Hester, throws herself under a truck and is decapitated. It was, Harding comes to feel,

> a Japanese-like suicide, a form of vengeance. Suppose you are a Japanese, and, on arriving home one evening, you find a corpse on your doorstep. You recognize it as that of a man with a grievance. You know that this man has taken his life in order to injure you. (*SC*, 395)

In this final structural permutation, then, the victim herself becomes the aggressor, absolving the satirist-subject and releasing him to this rather revolting expression of self-pity. It is not in fact a satisfactory solution. Harding's close relationship to Hester develops within the white or green silence of Lewis' most archetypcal room:

So they conversed, these two inmates of this lethal
chamber. Its depths were dark. Looked into from
without—by a contemplative bird established upon
the maple bough about a foot from the middle
window—the Hardings would have seemed (as they
moved about their circumscribed tasks, or rested
sluggishly upon the bottom as it were) provided with
an aquatic medium, lit where it grew dark by milky
bulbs . . . The green twilight that pervaded the lair
of the Hardings was composed of the coloration from
the wall of leaves of the summer maple, abetted by
the acrid green veil of the mosquito netting. Green
blinds latticed with use further contributed to this
effect of water, thickening the bloomy cavity. In
the winter a dark pallor, or the blue glare of the
snow, replaced the green. (*SC*, 174)

The intimacy enforced by this room ("you have become
integrated in me," Harding tells Hester, "this tête-à-tête of
ours over three years has made us as one person" [*SC*,
239]) stands somewhere between Tarr's onerous and intolerable liaison with Bertha and the emotional neutrality
of the purely masculine pseudocouple. But the narrative
apparatus of *Self Condemned* can no longer provide the
symbolic exchange and release of *Tarr*, and finds itself
obliged to dispose of the possessive mate by a violence
that obliterates the subject itself in the process. In this
novel, then, unconscious material rises dangerously close
to the surface. With that uncomfortable honesty so characteristic of him, Lewis here always seems on the point
of blurting out the truth, both to himself and to us; and
Self Condemned is surely the closest he ever came to self-
knowledge.

The same sexual *combinatoire*, meanwhile, can also explain the privileged place of *The Revenge for Love* in the
Lewis canon. This more openly political novel, by general
agreement his finest and most moving, draws its unaccustomed emotional resonance from a structural permutation
unique in Lewis' work: now for the first and last time, it
is from the woman's, from the victim's, point of view that

we are given to witness the deadly onslaught of the aggressive impulse. To be sure, the passive and victimized Margot marks no transcendence of the mature narrative system, which has no place for an anomalous figure like the Anastasya of *Tarr*. Margot's inner life is indeed as degraded as that of any of the puppets of *The Apes of God*, her intelligence poisoned and enfeebled by "Victorian lollypops" and by the genteelest fake watercolors from Ruskin to Virginia Woolf. She continues, moreover, to be rendered in the external and "satiric" mode which is that of the later fiction (but after *Tarr*, as we have seen, not even autobiographical figures like Harding or Pullman enjoy any unreserved authorial identification).

Still, the portrait of Margot is a kind of tour de force for Lewis: the collage composition remains the fundamental principle of construction of these sketches, which nonetheless piece their delicate and fragile object together with the swiftest abstract of bird movements:

> Her head of a small wistful seabird, delicately drafted to sail in the eye of the wind, and to skate upon the marbled surface of the waves—with its sleek feathery chevelure, in long matted wisps—arched downward on its neck to observe Lord Victor. The rhythm of his heaves, in his sulky imposture of sleep, certainly approximated the ocean. She hovered over him in her ecstasy of lovesickness, her eyes full of a dizzy gloating, rocked by the steady surge of his chest. Her eyes were almost popping out of her skull in the intensity of her desire to *settle*—to skim down and settle: to ride there and to be at rest! (*RL*, 62)

The now familiar informing presence of cliché—the collage of bird movements is not genuinely visual, but rather a gloss on the received idea of birds "settling"—does not to be sure break through into the plenitude of artificial epic; nonetheless, it may be taken as something of a dialectical "negation of the negation" in the way in which the externality of the dominant satiric portraiture in Lewis is here systematically undermined. Here is Margot standing up:

> She waxed wanly, indeed, very nervelessly but airily—becoming a full-length, also, with a certain loss of ground, giving away a foot or so as she drifted upwards. As a plant, as it rose into the air, falling away from the prevalent quarter of the wind, so she fell away before the face of her recumbent lord—with eyes inevitably lowered, and hand behind her upon the back of her chair. (*RL*, 64)

This is evidently the attempt to generate a cliché which would be the gestural contrary of "settling," a "falling away" that rises vertically: just as in a more general way, the character of Margot is an attempt to readapt the techniques of satiric externality to a figure which is the structural inversion of its customary degraded and mechanical content.

Nor can Victor really be considered a new and positive figure for Lewis either. If Harding marks the final destiny of the Tarr-ego in Lewis' post-World-War-I narrative system, then Victor must be seen as the equally unexpected avatar of the old Kreisler-id. Unlike Tarr, Victor is the very prototype of the *bad* artist; like Kreisler, he is an outsider, and as an Australian emits the signal of some strenuous and predominantly physical existence. "His attitude towards the world," one of the characters tells us, "is what, if he were a Great Power, would be called typically that of the *Have-Not*—I use the current jargon of the press. . . . Victor, I think, suffers from an inferiority—complex. . . . Oh, yes. Victor is very like Germany!" (*RL*, 224). Yet Victor has none of the violent and self-destructive characteristics that made Kreisler such a striking figure: his structural position as the Pariah—the combination of Strength and Non-Intelligence—rather marks him out for the role of the sacrificial victim.

What saves these figures from becoming the merest puppets of satiric representation—in the framework of *The*

Apes of God this particular combination of Bloomsbury bad taste and of bad painting would be an ominous sign indeed—is the coincidence, in the person of their enemies, of the sexual-instinctual and the political levels of Lewis' imagination. The villains are thus at one and the same time Marxists, Bohemian fellow-travellers, false intellectuals, and men of *ressentiment* and misogynists out to take a conspicuous and exemplary "revenge for love":

> It was *their* reality, that of Victor and herself, that was marked down to be discouraged and abolished, and it was *they* that the others were trying to turn into phantoms and so to suppress. It was a mad notion, but it was just as if they had engaged in a battle of wills, to decide who should possess most *reality*— just as men fought each other for money, or fought each other for food. (*RL,* 158)

The political fantasy-structure (the Marxists are out to destroy "individuality") allows Lewis to dissociate himself from the aggressive impulse, which is now attributed to the enemy (what we have previously identified as the "diabolical" term). With this transfer of guilt—the only successful such operation in Lewis—for the first and last time genuine emotion, a real sympathy and feeling for the victims, is unexpectedly released.

The tragic end of Victor and Margot in the Spain of the early 1930's must have seemed something of a historical aberration, when, in the early days of the Spanish Civil War, the novel finally appeared. And in fact it is an anomaly in Lewis' production: what will be retained from it in Lewis' later work is not its sympathy with the victims, but rather precisely the conspiratorial motif itself, which a remarkable generic enlargement—what we have called theological science fiction—is called on to justify and formally to legitimate.

The figure of the Bailiff indeed includes and recapitulates within itself every conceivable feature and variation of

Lewis' political and social polemics: radicalism, *ressentiment*, homosexuality, feminist sympathies, the Time Cult, the Youth Cult, even artistic modernism (the background music at the Bailiff's cocktail parties turns out to be Alban Berg's *Lyric Suite*). As one might suspect, he thereby becomes Lewis' most lively character. Nonetheless, the function of the villain is so conventional and so thoroughly ideological, so fundamentally inseparable from ethical stereotypes and from that binary axis of Good and Evil, of which Nietzsche long ago recommended the demolition, that it is difficult to revive without interesting and unsuspected structural modifications. The theological thriller, as it plays itself out from Graham Greene to LeCarre, proposed a simple but effective reversal, in which it is the villains (Graham Greene's sinful, guilt-ridden Catholics, LeCarre's East Germans) who turn out to embody the positive term, while the stereotypical heroes (healthy athletic protestants or clean-cut American Cold Warriors) are unmasked as the agents of evil and human suffering.

In *The Human Age*, the villains remain, but the opposing positive term finds itself unexpectedly emptied of its ethical content. Lewis' white angels are for one thing, not human agents, but the supports and bearers of sheer energy: they no longer function therefore as characters in the ordinary sense, even though their anthropomorphic appearance permits the narrativization of the otherwise unrepresentable material of transindividual forces. Lewis, who felt more comfortable with categories of race rather than with those of social class, here projects his vision of the struggle of political powers into the narrative apparatus of distinct supernatural species: white angels, fallen angels, minor demons born of the mating of the angels with the "daughters of men." The vision effectively heals the rift between political and instinctual codes: the biological vested interests of these various species can be read indifferently as either instinctual or political. Better still, in this peculiar afterlife, Lewis' sexual politics dictate the terms in which political struggle itself is acted out, while his view of the political as a fundamentally nonmoral calculus of sheer power empties this "theology" of any conceivable ethical content.

We may say this another way, and thereby distance Lewis' theoretical science fiction from contemporary work in this form with which it has sometimes been compared (Chesterton, David Lindsay, C. S. Lewis, Charles Williams), by observing that his is an afterlife utterly lacking in transcendence. It is, indeed, as we have already noted, a resolutely materialistic one: "There is no such thing as the supernatural," the Devil remarks authoritatively to Pullman (*MF*, 62); and the latter gradually comes to understand that in a cosmos in which "evil" and "good" are simply measurable and material quantities of force, the whole matter of piety and impiety resolves itself into an assessment of the balance of power.

God is thus but one powerful angel among many, and the conflicts in this afterworld are little more moral (but no less ideological) than those of the Cold War. Pullman's philosophical problem, therefore, the problem of "man," very rapidly transforms itself into the dilemma of finding some adequate shelter or hiding place for the human subject in the superhuman conflict between these vast forces.

His ultimate enlistment on the side of God is thus a political rather than a moral conversion, and does not so much suggest that Pullman has seen through Sammael's program—much of which he devised himself—as rather that God has finally proved to be the more powerful of the two opposing parties. Yet the political intrigue of *The Human Age* presents the added advantage of allowing Lewis to dissect the strategy of the Devil's party in the now familiar ethico-historical ones of his journalistic polemics. There is now therefore no longer any Good; yet the Devil's program remains evil. Just as the Bailiff, in his relatively more local way, systematically attempted to undermine the last vestiges of any autonomous human individuality, so now the reforms of the Devil—the promotion of the new "human age" itself, the shrinking of the angels to human size and to a human life-span, worse yet, their introduction to a more properly human *temporality*— all these projects are now understood to spring from the Devil's *ressentiment,* from some boundless "revenge for the divine" which aims at nothing less than the utter subversion of the angelic nature.

There can thus, in this curious work, be no question of any genuine religious experience as this is normally understood. The "God" of *The Human Age* has little enough to do with the ways in which traditional religions have projected their visions of divinity or of the sacred. Lewis' own religious position, indeed, as he describes it in a striking page of *Time and Western Man,* gives the impression of a negative theology refracted through the narrow lens of Lewis' conception of satiric externality:

> We are surface-creatures, and the 'truths' from beneath the surface contradict our values. It is among the flowers and the leaves that our lot is cast, and the roots, however 'interesting', are not so ultimate for us. . . . For us the ultimate thing is the surface, the last-comer, and that is committed to a plurality of being. . . . We think it is most true and better to say there is *no* God. To us the practical requirements seem to indicate the contrary of Kant's pragmatic solution—to require the conception of a Many instead of a One. On the other hand, if anything, the speculative reason seems to us to point to a One. But on the One we must turn our back in order to exist. . . . It is *we* who have to pretend to be real, if any one has to, not to pretend that God is.
>
> (*TWM,* 387–388)

The concept of God—the Logic of traditional theology, the place of meditation on the Ideas of perfection, infinity, and Being—thus offers no relief for Lewis' anxieties about the stability of the ego and the reality of individual life but tends, if anything, to exasperate them.

Nor can this "theology" be assimilated to that experience of the sacred, which, under the form of magic, constitutes the ideological expression of tribal society before the emergence of political power and institutionalized priesthoods: for the magical impulse had already, as we have seen, found a more purely secular embodiment in generalized satiric aggressivity.

Yet something of the religious tradition is peculiarly reinvented in *The Human Age*, which seems anachronistically to prolong that patristic and medieval speculation on the angelic nature which was so thoroughly ridiculed and discredited by Enlightenment rationalism. It is not certain that such apparently senseless meditations are religious in any traditional meaning of the word, even though, as in Augustine or Thomas Aquinas, they may be woven into the systematic presentation of the theological treatise. Rather, the reflection on the angelic nature is of a piece with the attempt to imagine the experience of human life before the Fall, or to envision Paradise. From the hindsight of the modern Utopian tradition, from Fourier to Marcuse and Ernst Bloch, we may suggest that such thinking is an attempt to expand the hegemonic religious code to accommodate what is essentially a vision of the Utopian body, of the libidinal transfiguration of human life in some nonalienated state.

Lewis' angels thus retain their instinctual content but dramatize the formal dilemma of the Utopian imagination itself, which must open a space for itself beyond this fallen world of contingency, to which however its categories remain corporeally shackled. The truth of the Utopian imagination indeed may be said to lie not in the representations it achieves, but rather ultimately in its failure to imagine its object; the greatest Utopias are thus those which, dramatizing the limits and the impoverishment of our visions of Utopia, denounce the imprisonment of the reading mind in the asphyxiating immanence of its here-and-now.[2] This dialectic of the imagination returning critically upon itself and its own limits takes other forms in Lewis as well, however, as we shall see in our concluding chapter.

In the perspective of a libidinal Utopia, however, it is scarcely surprising that the crux of Lewis' "reflection" on the angelic nature should be the question of angelic sexuality. As meaningless as such a "problem" may seem from a rationalistic or scientific standpoint, it has always had political significance in periods whose hegemonic code or ideological language was religious, and in which issues that the secular mind would identify as social or political ones must necessarily express themselves in those coded or symbolic terms which constitute the only sign-system available. Christopher Hill has in fact observed that the alternate positions on whether the angels are or are not sexual provide a reliable touchstone for determining the political and ideological orientation of precapitalist intellectuals.[3]

2. See, on this movement of the utopian imagination, my "World Reduction in LeGuin: The Emergence of Utopian Narrative," in *Science-Fiction Studies* 7, Vol. II, No. 3 (November, 1975), pp. 221–230; and "Of Islands and Trenches: Neutralization and the Production of Utopian Discourse," in *Diacritics* (June, 1977), pp. 2–21.

3. "One consequence of belief in the goodness of matter, and of Milton's rejection of dualism, was his insistence on the corporeality of angels, which upsets some readers of *Paradise Lost*. Not only do they 'shed tears such as angels weep'; they also bleed, eat, digest, excrete, blush and interpenetrate sexually, though in a suitably angelic manner. (We recall R. O.'s pleasantries about 'an evacuating soul' in *Mans Mortalitie*, his object being the same as Milton's,—to deny the separation of soul and body. Clarkson and Muggleton made the same point: the soul eats and drinks.) Milton's heresies about angels eating and digesting (not 'in mist, the common gloss/ Of theologians'—*P.L.* V, 434–8) seem only to be fully paralleled in Fludd, though there are suggestions in Sylvester/Du Bartas and Boehme; the radical John Webster later proclaimed, in opposition to Henry More, that angels had bodies. The doctrine is ancient, but by the seventeenth century it was associated with the magical, Hermeticist/Paracelsan tradition; it was accepted by the Baptist Henry Lawrence, Robert Gell, Hobbes, Hale

Lewis' angels, as befits this essentially conservative or reactionary thinker, are, not surprisingly, sexless and project an attempt to imagine a life liberated from sex and from desire. Thus the Devil tells us that his own "fall from heaven," grievously misrepresented in the human press, was in reality his own initiative and amounted to slamming the door in disgust when God took it upon himself to create Woman. Sammael's subversion of the divine therefore has as its fundamental strategy the introduction of women and sex into angelic existence. "What has to be proved," comments Pullman, as adviser to this diabolical enterprize, "is whether the angels' genitals, extinct for so many thousands of years, are not extinct for good" (*MF*, 163).

To imagine angels is therefore here an impossible attempt to imagine a world beyond sex. Lewis' angels—save for immense celestial catfights—are energy stilled, energy concentrated, yet unimaginably slowed down, in obedience to vaster rhythms or cycles than those of the time of human existence. As we have already noted, what characterizes such celestial bureaucrats as the Padishah, the angelic governor of Third City, is the effortless and astonishing plenitude with which they realize the ancient Epicurean dream of *ataraxia* or sheer indifference:

> [Pullman] attempted to penetrate the veil of this immortal, who passed his days in isolation, since there was no one good enough, or supernatural enough, for him to communicate with. What dreams had he at night? Perhaps he flew, with great wings, through the golden skies of Heaven; or imagined the arrival of an angelic visitor, to whom be might unburden himself. The emotion which appeared to sweep across him incessantly, and which obviously originated in wells of unfathomable boredom, to be found somewhere at the centre of his being, produced the facial expres-

---

and Gilbert Burnet. Conservatives like Donne and Sir William Davenant specifically denied sex to angels. Milton wanted to relate his angels closely to men and women, and to proclaim the dignity of sex."—Christopher Hill, *Milton and the English Revolution* (New York: Viking, 1978), pp. 331–332.

sion which remained, above all else, in Pullman's
memory. . . . Clearly everything to do with Man
filled him with an immense fatigue, a passionate lack
of interest.   (*MG*, 129–130)

Sex is therefore but the most concentrated expression of
everything which repels the angelic mind about human nature: of the intensely personal, passionate, grappling nature of human desires and longings and of human involve-
ments. Nothing dramatizes this repulsion more strikingly
than the erratic behavior of the celestial messenger who
comes to warn Pullman that his anti-God activities are
well known in Heaven:

> Returning to the Haus Europa after several hours
> spent at the Sports Centre, Pullman opened the door
> of his flat and discovered a tall white figure engaged
> in fixing something upon his wall. It was one of the
> dreaded angels. As he entered the room the heavenly
> messenger stepped back from the wall and began
> gliding towards the windows. The creature did not
> move very quickly; indeed it was with a strange som-
> nambulistic lassitude that this White Angel propelled
> himself towards a likely exit. Pullman's energy was as
> great as the angel's was small; so small, indeed, as to
> appear to suffer from a debility which invaded all his
> muscles and caused him to drag himself along. Now
> the more galvanic of these two rushed to the window,
> reaching it before the intruder, locking it and remov-
> ing the key. Charged as he was with will, Pullman
> shrank from the pallid, inhuman being, whose face
> glared emptily and was as incapable of fear as of any-
> thing else. That creature of a mysterious flesh showed
> no signs of alarm. This was not a frightened bird,
> attempting to escape from a room into which it had
> blundered, but the bearer of a terrible message, who
> did not wish for any contact with this evil man. This
> in no way nonplussed visitor, beginning to glide as
> heavily as before, turned doorwards. . . .
>
> (*MF*, 203–204)

The angelic nature, "imagined" negatively, and represent-
able only in terms of the privation of human desires and

energies, provides an unexpected solution to a narrative dilemma which is also an ideological and instinctual contradiction: for it stands at one and the same time as a negation *both* of the human *and* of the diabolical, both of the suppression of sex by the hypertrophied ego, and of its threatening release in the form of aggressivity and *ressentiment*. This is a space which is from the point of view of the Freudian topology "U-topian" in the strict sense of the term: neither ego nor id, neither sex nor its repression.

In a society in which consumers' goods have been relentlessly sexualized, and in which sex has itself become a commodity, this once reactionary motif in Lewis' work—which inscribed itself in willful contradiction across all the liberatory struggles against puritanism and sexual hypocrisy in his own period—may now no longer have quite the same resonance. Marcuse has shown us how those older images of sexual and instinctual gratification which had such explosive negative and critical force in Victorian society have in a "postindustrial" *société de consommation*, which no longer needs the cement of sexual taboo, been harnessed to the service of the status quo and consumerism in the form of what he calls "repressive desublimation."[4] Indeed, his own Utopia foresees a dimunition in overt sexual preoccupations in proportion to the increasing erotization of the work and of the object-world of the Utopian community.

Lewis' vision of angelic indifference may provide us with a kind of strange stillness in which to sense this alien, unimaginable reality, a disturbing silence in which we may seem to have been granted some glimpse into our own reality transfigured:

> All along that side of Angeltown, bordering the vast
> empty space reserved for their manoeuvres, silent,
> the giant citizenry stood, higher than any but the
> loftiest mountains, light clouds resting on their

4. Herbert Marcuse, *One-Dimensional Man* (Boston: Beacon Press, 1964), pp. 72–79.

shoulders, their faces as unemotional as the hardest
material of the earth, their tiny houses collected at
their feet. (*MF, 215*)

It is a silence that cannot last: into the very heart of this
Utopian fantasy, reality implacably reinserts itself, impos-
ing its irrevocable dynamism.

The Human Age may be thought of as an imaginative
attempt to bracket or suspend the contingencies of a fallen
history and a material present. The story it has to tell is
then the unavoidable return of everything thus initially repressed by the apparatus of representation. So we witness
a world without women or sex, into which the latter are
systematically reintroduced; a world without economics, a
kind of cosmic welfare state, with its government-issued
stamp-script, in which the most vicious blackmarket practices begin to flourish; a world beyond the reach of human
actions and human powers, in which nonetheless the four
great earthly political forces—Communism, fascism, the
church, *Realpolitik*—continue their eternal combat as on
earth.

At length, in the timelessness of the eternal, History
itself makes its fatal reappearance. Nothing in *The Human
Age* is quite so striking as the way in which, at this point,
Lewis' system of representation approaches something like
a genuine dialectical consciousness of itself. It presupposed
the familiar cosmology of the Christian tradition, with its
Heaven and Hell, its God and Devil, its angels and human
souls awaiting judgement. Yet this cosmology is itself a
historical representation, bound to the specificity of a
long-since vanished medieval culture. Thus when Pullman
seeks to adjust the strangely contemporary reality of Third
City to this archaic cosmological system, he is given an
astonishing explanation:

> Before the modern age, yes, back in the Age of Faith,
> there was a Heaven and there was a Hell. There was
> a Heaven of dazzling white, and there was a good
> coal-black Hell. Now, to arrange, somewhere in

space, a convenient site for these institutions was not
too easy in those days. . . . Hell and Heaven are
much too near geographically, and the same applies
to Third City—that is much too near to Hell. . . .
Hell is just over there. Things have progressed as
they have down on earth. These opposites are far too
near together for modern conditions. . . . Heaven is
no longer immaculate—is it?. . . . Hell is not the
place it once was in the days of our old friend Dante
Alighierei . . . You saw perhaps that performance
[the visit of a diplomatic mission from Hell to Third
City] down on Fifth Piazza this afternoon? They were
a terrible crew weren't they? But that was a beauty
chorus Lucifer keeps for such occasions to frighten
the bourgeoisie. It is a little family or two of genuine,
old-time devils, who live in the wilds of Hades, just
as the elk lives up in the Bush, as far from man as
possible. These demons are rounded up when they
are required. . . . As we all know, and can see for
ourselves, the *Good* and the *Bad* are blurred, are they
not, in the modern age? We no longer see things in
stark black and white. We know that all men are
much the same. An amoralist. . . . such is the
modern man. And in the same way in these supernatural regions. It is a terrible come-down all round.
What was once the Devil (to whom one 'sold one's
soul' and so forth) well today, he is a very unconvinced *devil*, and our Padishah, as we call him, he is a
very unconvinced Angel. (*MG*, 112–113)

The modification of Dante's cosmology, the insertion of
the bureaucratic welfare state of Third City in between the
more archaic traditional sites of Heaven and Hell, marks
the approach of this system of representation to something
like an immanent awareness of its own historicity, to a
virtual thematization of its own conditions of possibility
and of the historical and cultural impossibility of reviving
and imagining the medieval cosmos from the standpoint of
contemporary life. Yet this impossibility, which threatens
to undermine the representational frame which allowed us
to be aware of it in the first place, is then itself drawn back
within the system of representation where, as the hypothe-

sis of change and "progress" in the afterlife, it becomes yet another feature of the represented object.

At this point, Hell and Heaven are posited as having a history of their own, and Paradise comes to be seen as a civilization entering a stage of historical degeneration and anarchy much like the great Mogul or Manchu empires during the European eighteenth century. Third City, Pullman is told, "is the decay of an at one time more sensible system. . . . They had somehow found their way, posthumously, into a decayed sub-celestial system, on the eve of destruction by infernal agency" (MG, 24, 26). So the imagination of Lewis, intent on freeing itself from the "nightmares of history," finds itself, in obedience to its own rigorous logic and that of its raw material, unable to keep from reinventing them, and arrives in Heaven just in time to witness under way there a repetition of the same dismal process of cultural corruption that it had denounced on earth.

9/
HOW TO DIE TWICE

With the human, death is found a very short distance
beneath the surface.

Malign Fiesta

OREMOST AMONG SUCH STUBBORNLY
recurrent facts is that of death itself: the
attempt to imagine death is at the ideological and instinctual center of *The Human Age*. This proposition, however,
cannot be fully explored, let alone eval-
uated, unless we presuppose from the outset that "real"
death is for all of us rigorously unimaginable: the images
and representations by which we seem to have achieved
some tangible certainty as to the nature of death must from
that standpoint be supposed, a priori, to be so many de-
flections. But if this is so, then representations of death
will always prove, under closer inspection, to be complex
displacements of an indirect, symbolic meditation about
something else.

This is the sense in which death in *The Human Age*
may be seen as the "final solution" to a quite different and

fundamentally ideological dilemma which haunted Lewis throughout his life, namely, the problem of "personality" and the contradiction between this supreme value and the satiric apparatus which Lewis evolved for its defense. Such contradictions (or more properly, such antinomies) can always be reformulated in terms of a question, to which the narrative then appears to provide the answer: it being understood that the question is in fact unanswerable, and that the narrative "answer" is in reality a kind of sleight of hand.

It is indeed as though Lewis were asking himself how it is possible for people who are not really alive—the mass-produced simulacra of modern civilization, the sham puppet-victims of his satire—to die. In what sense can death be real if life itself has been unreal? The question is not mere abstract metaphysical speculation but is intensely charged with the guilt of Lewis' formal practice as a satirist, a role which, as we have seen, is constitutively informed by an aggressivity trained on those very objects whose reality is now in question. To put it another way, if it can be shown that death itself is unreal, if it follows logically from the premises of the question asked above that people who were never really alive in the first place cannot really die either, then the satirist is absolved of all his guilt for victims who have only undergone an appearance of death, and not its irrevocable reality. The apparatus of theological science fiction, then, from its initial volume in 1928, has the welcome consequence of assuring Lewis that his victims never really died and indeed can never do so ("the masses of personalities, whom God, having created them, is unable to destroy"). So also in the later volumes, apparently disturbing spectacles, such as the view of "souls" grievously maimed or squashed in accidents, mere vegetables which are however indestructible, and preserved forever in drawers specially manufactured for the purpose—such spectacles in reality serve as reas-

suring narrative proof of what was to have been demonstrated in the first place, namely that Lewis' satire never
killed anyone and could never do so.

Yet at this point something unaccountable begins to
take place: as *The Human Age* progresses, it becomes only
too clear that the resurrected dead of this afterlife can
really die after all, and this time for good, in the horrors of
Lewis' Auschwitz-Hell. Nor is this unexpected mortality a
merely local, human accident but rather spreads irrevoca-
bly throughout the whole length and breadth of this henceforth material cosmos. Thus the very angels, as physical as
human beings in their own way, can be destroyed fully as
effectively as the more fragile human "sinners": so that a
perspective emerges at the end of which an ultimate possibility is glimpsed—the eventual mortality and extinction
of the Devil, and even of God himself.

This unexpected reversal confirms the contradictory
structure of Lewis' original object of meditation: a turning
mechanism whose reverse slope the narrative imagination
must now descend. In the logic of fantasy-thought, the experience of death became indissolubly linked to the problem of the "reality" of life, or in other words, the existence
and substantiality of the strong "personality." The negative answer freed the satirist from guilt: his objects were
not "personalities" in this sense, and so he could in no way
be supposed to have destroyed them. Yet the affirmation
of the ideological value of "personality" as such demands
that this negative answer be reduplicated by a positive one
which contradicts it at all points: from this angle, then,
only the prospect of genuine death can confirm the reality
of individual existence. Only if death is real after all, can
the existence of the "strong personality" be firmly and ir-
refutably established.

The climactic scene of *The Revenge for Love* in effect
provided a first trial run for the attempt to imagine death
in all its once-and-for-all irrevocability. We have already
examined the complicated strategy whereby Lewis uses

Margot's limited and inadequate representation of death to project the place of the thing-in-itself which can by definition never achieve representation within the monad. Margot's images are both maintained and cancelled out, deleted by some Heideggerian or Derridean "erasure" which nonetheless confirms and preserves the status of those impoverished images as the only vehicle available for what can otherwise be neither seen nor said.

The Human Age now dialectically intensifies this peculiar operation, transforming it in the process into a qualitatively new and higher narrative solution. In retrospect, its elements already seem to have been implicit in the instinctual content of *Self Condemned:*

> The fact was that René Harding had stood up to
> the Gods, when he resigned his professorship in
> England. The Gods had struck him down. They had
> humiliated him, made him a laughing stock, cut him
> off from all recovery; they had driven him into the
> wilderness. The hotel fire gave him a chance of a
> second lease of life. He seized it with a mad alacrity;
> he was not, he had not been, killed—he had survived
> the first retaliatory blow—the expulsion, the ostra-
> cism. . . . When the Gods struck the second time
> there was, from the moment of the blow, and the
> days spent in the white silence of the hospital, no
> chance that he could survive, at all intact. You can-
> not kill a man twice, the Gods cannot strike *twice* and
> the man survive.   (*SC*, 406)

In effect, in this context *Self Condemned* offers a demonstration not unlike that of a fable like "The Boy Who Wanted to Learn Fear." It is as though, when the imagination of death fails you on some primary level, its commonplace or stereotypical representations need to be repeated, worked through, and exhausted by a narrative which, having taken you through death unsuccessfully a first time, can now recuperate this failure by bringing the reading mind up short against the unpremeditated shock of a *second* dying. This process can be observed at its starkest and most effective in Ambrose Bierce's "An Occurrence at Owl Creek Bridge," where the survival flashback endows the condemned man's "second" drop with all the grisly force of "real" neck-breaking gravity. The theological framework of *The Human Age* can now be understood as providing a system in which such narrative reduplication is available in a non-linear way, a system which provides for the survival of the puppet-victims of the "real world" of satire, only the better to ensure the definitive finality, in that material afterworld that replicates it, of their *second death*.

With the peculiar overdetermination of this narrative framework, our analysis of *The Human Age* would seem to have reached some ultimate limit, an incomprehensible given, an arbitrary starting point, beyond which it cannot pass. Yet the resonance which the phenomenon of "second death" has found in Lacanian psychoanalysis suggests a further line of speculation and interpretation, at the cost of a brief detour through the latter. Lacan himself discovered the motif in Sade; and it is appropriate that his interpretation of it in terms of the late Freudian "death wish" should offer a final occasion to confront Lewis' energy model with the Freudian one with which we have so frequently, but only incidentally, compared it.

Lacan's reading of the phenomenon of the imagination of "second death" has consequences for two distinct areas, both of which are relevant to Lewis: "second death" dramatizes the subject's problematic relationship to its own desire, yet it also has a revealing part to play in our essentially conflictual relationships to other subjects (Lacan's "mirror stage" and behind it the Hegelian Master/Slave struggle for recognition).

The apparent irrelevance of the problem of desire to what is essentially a vision of death (or, in Sade, a pursuit of suffering) is clarified by the late Freudian conception of the death wish as an instinct, and a form of "desire," fully as powerful and as goal-oriented as Eros itself. We must also understand that for Lacan, no less than for Freud himself, desire or the "wish" is a drive that can never be satisfied, but only momentarily stilled. In our own framework, which is that of narrative analysis, the justification for this otherwise seemingly metaphysical proposition is of the greatest interest: for Freud and Lacan, desire necessarily emerges in a "bound" state, that is, inextricably invested in a determinate representation, or fantasy-structure, or instinctual "narrative" or "text" (the so-called *Vorstellungsrepräsentanz,* or "ideational representative"). There are in this sense no pure instincts or impulses, which then search about for the appropriate real or imaginary objects. As far back as one can go in the psyche, desire always presents itself as already crystallized or articulated in a particular figuration. This is why the acting out of desire can never be successful: however literal the real-life replay, there must always persist a structural, one would even want to say, an ontological, incommensurability between the "text" of desire and the "reality" of the subject's enactment of it: whatever the latter is, and however physically gratifying, it is never the same as the fantasy-text or scenario of which it wishes to be the definitive performance.

Now the privileged place of a work like Sade's can be understood: Sade's work—and at a lower level, pornography generally—amounts to something like a recognition of this structural gap between the text of desire and its reenactment, which in its turn it attempts to overcome by transforming the latter back into a written text. Yet the exemplary value of Sade, in contrast to ordinary or first-level pornography, lies in the way in which the text unexpectedly foregrounds this process, which it recognizes as an impossibility.

The appearance of the motif of "second death" is just such a privileged moment in Sade's work and accompanies the discovery of a peculiar contradiction in the behavior of one of his principal figures, the torturer-executioner

Saint-Fond. The latter's feminine accomplices are insistent on finding out why he always first "shuts himself up for an hour with [the individual marked out for torture and death]; it seemed that at such moments the libertine was in the process of transmitting some impenetrable secret to his victim, which the latter was being instructed to carry with him into the other world."[1] It transpires, to the astonishment of his listeners—all atheists and materialists of the most intransigent Enlightenment variety—that Saint-Fond actually believes in the afterlife; during such absences, he takes pains to assure his victim eternal damnation as well as physical death, thus procuring "the delicious pleasure of prolonging [the victim's suffering] beyond the very limits of eternity, if eternity has any."[2]

Lacan's comment on this episode runs as follows:

> The idea of hell, over and over refuted by [Sade] and stigmatized as the legitimating instrument of religious tyranny, now curiously returns to motivate the gestures of that one of his heroes who is among the most passionately committed to libertine subversion in its philosophical, Enlightenment form. . . . The methods used to inflict the ultimate penalty on his victims are grounded on the belief that he can render their agony eternal in the beyond. The authenticity of this conduct is then underscored by his attempts to conceal it from his accomplices as well as by his embarrassment at explaining it to them. . . . This incoherence in Sade. . . . may be accounted for by the term "second death" formally pronounced by him. The security he expects [this two-fold murder] to provide him against the horrible routine of nature (to interrupt which is according to him the very function of crime itself) requires the prolongation of death to the point at which the swooning of the subject in orgasm is itself reduplicated: this reduplication is then given symbolic form in the wish [expressed in Sade's

---

1. D. A. F. de Sade, *L'Histoire de Juliette,* in *Oeuvres complètes* (Paris: Cercle du livre précieux, 1966), Vol. VIII, p. 354.
2. Ibid., p. 357.

last will and testament as well as in the horrors
inflicted by his characters on the dead bodies of their
victims] that the decomposed elements of our bodies
be utterly annihilated in order to prevent them from
rejoining anew.[3]

"Second death" is thus here taken as an index of the way
in which desire, exasperated by the unsatisfying immedi-
acy of its nominal fulfillment in the here-and-now, seeks
perpetually to transcend itself, and to project the mirage
and the "beyond" of a fuller imaginary satisfaction upon
the horizon and beyond the "reality" of its sheerly physical
enactment.

But we have not yet specified the connection between
this transcendent dynamic within desire and the enigmatic
Freudian death wish. It will already have been understood
that, however the concept is interpreted, it would be a
serious misconception to reduce it immediately to a longing for "real" death, or to assimilate it too rapidly to such
feelings as morbid despondency or suicidal depression. It
is best initially to grasp the Thanatos as a prolongation of
the aims of its opposite number, Eros, by other and more
extreme means. Better still, the Thanatos must be seen in
a different light when we understand that Eros also is essentially a negative rather than a positive drive, and that
the pleasure principle aims less at positive satisfaction than
at the removal of tension: "unpleasure corresponds to an
increase in the quantity of excitation and pleasure to a *di-
minution*."[4] It is as though Thanatos, exasperated by the

3. Jacques Lacan, "Kant avec Sade," in *Écrits* (Paris: Seuil, 1966), p. 776.
4. Sigmund Freud, *Beyond the Pleasure Principle*, in the Standard Edition
(London: Hogarth Press, 1955), Volume XVIII, p. 8. It will shortly become
clear that on my reading the Eros/Thanatos distinction corresponds to the current French distinction between "plaisir" and "jouissance." Freud's own hesi-
tations ("what follows is speculation, often far-fetched speculation, which the
reader will consider or dismiss according to his individual predilection" [p. 24])
perhaps entitle us to suggest that his own reinterpretation of the Thanatos in
terms of an innate instinct of aggression is fully as ideological as that of his later
commentators.

half-measures of Eros, whose momentary satisfactions merely result in the inevitable return of just those tensions and excitations it was supposed to lay to rest, now decided to go all the way with the latter's program, and to apply it so thoroughly that the irritation of organic life would once and for all be made an end to: "it seems," Freud tells us in a famous passage,

> that an instinct is an urge inherent in organic life to restore an earlier state of things which the living entity has been obliged to abandon under the pressure of external disturbing forces; that is, it is a kind of organic elasticity, or, to put it another way, the expression of the inertia inherent in organic life. . . . Instincts are therefore bound to give a deceptive appearance of being forces tending towards change and progress, whilst in fact they are merely seeking to reach an ancient goal by paths alike old and new. Moreover it is possible to specify this final goal of organic striving. . . . It must be an *old* state of things, an initial state from which the living entity has at one time or other departed and to which it is striving to return by the circuitous paths along which its development leads. If we are to take it as a truth that knows no exception that everything living dies for *internal* reasons—becomes inorganic again—then we shall be compelled to say that *'the aim of all life is death'* and, looking backwards, that *'inanimate things existed before living ones'*. . . . For a long time, perhaps, living substance was thus being constantly created afresh and easily dying, till decisive external influences altered in such a way as to oblige the still living substance to diverge ever more widely from its original course of life and to make ever more complicated *detours* before reaching its aim of death.[5]

If we want to read this passage properly, we must, at the risk of crudeness, replace Freud's biological language with a more overt specification of the sexual content evidently implicit in it. No less than Eros, the Thanatos also has

5. Ibid., pp. 36, 38–39.

orgasm as its ultimate aim and end. Only where Eros marks a kind of realistic compromise, a consent to time and an accommodation to the inevitable rebirth and organic repetition of desire, Thanatos projects an otherwise more final solution and wills, as it were, to come so completely that desire and sex utterly cease to exist and their intolerable repetition is forever silenced. The ideal of the Thanatos, the "death" which is the object of the death wish, is thus something quite different from physical mortality: its supreme aim is rather *aphanasis*, asexuality, the radical extinction of sexual desire itself, that serene and inorganic indifference of which Lewis' angels give us so vivid a representation.

Life, of course, can only fulfill this wish by way of a fatal misinterpretation, which substitutes the extinction of the subject itself for the extinction of its desire. The dynamics of Thanatos are more properly visible in the imaginary and its texts, as the perpetual projection of another, and radically different, space in which the implacable demand of the death wish for some total and ultimate satisfaction, manifestly unavailable in the everyday "real" world of Eros, may finally be met. Thus Sade registers his dissatisfaction with the banal and conventionalized practices of real-life perversion by powerfully opening a textual and imaginary space in which the person and the acts of Saint-Fond can more completely realize them. Yet at this point, at which the text of Sade would remain indistinguishable from representational pornography of the standard type,[6] something unexpected happens: Sade's inaugural gesture of transcendence finds itself reduplicated

6. There is however a principle of transcendence in first-level or representational pornography, ordinarily misconceived as "transgression," which inscribes itself on a kind of hierarchy of sexual codes which "rise" from normal sex through rape, gang bangs, incest, Nabokov's nympholatry, homosexuality, sado-masochism, etc. The reader's text is always "marked" as difference or as a text, by dramatizing the next code up the ladder from his own sexual behavior; meanwhile, in consumer society, the series is developed diachronically as successive taboos are systematically exploited and "exhausted."

within his own textual representation, and Saint-Fond—
reproducing Sade's dissatisfaction within his own reality
(now Sade's representation)—repeats the latter's gesture of
transcendence and opens up a text beyond the text itself,
a textual "beyond" or afterlife in which ultimate, transcendent satisfaction is to be imagined. Saint-Fond's ideal
of the "second death" thus marks Sade's episode as autoreferential, reproducing within the representation itself
Sade's own relationship to it.

As for the other feature of the "second death," its
function in the subject's relations with other subjects, this
too must be understood as something quite distinct from
the conventional notions of "sadism" or of aggressivity
conceived as some primary instinct:

> If one interprets the Imaginary relationship as a
> Hegelian struggle for recognition as Lacan does, then
> one understands that the 'struggle for pure prestige'
> in the Imaginary cannot depend on any kind of real
> death. It is in effect dependent on an implicit or un-
> conscious pact between the participants: that they
> shall both survive, for one cannot be recognized
> alone. The dialectic must therefore depend on
> *IMAGINED* death . . .[7]

Yet in the realm of aesthetic representation, in which
everything is imaginary in this sense, such exemplary texts
as those of Sade or Lewis reveal this process to have a
well-nigh infinite dynamic: the figure you kill is already
imaginary, so that for this first-level representation a second must be substituted—an imaginary of the Imaginary
itself—and for that second one, yet another, and so forth,
in a regression which has no end. Lewis' satire aimed at
killing organic reality and endowing it with the spatial
stasis of the visual: but in this Hegelian struggle with the
living reality which is satire's object, the victory must remain an imaginary one. So that initial reality projects itself

---

7. A. G. Wilden, *System and Structure* (London: Tavistock, 1972), pp. 468–
469.

into a phantom and transcendent realm beyond its own material remains, in order there the more surely to die a second time.

We cannot leave this description, however, without observing that the psychoanalytic framework is an essentially ahistorical one, which posits the dynamics of the "second death," or of the death wish, as a permanent feature of human existence since its origins. However this may be, it is clear that such dynamics are peculiarly intensified by that process of reification which differentiates our social life from that of every other social formation in human history and which is uniquely specific to capitalism as a mode of production. Reification exasperates the relationship of desire to its objects to the point where the dialectic of representation discussed above knows a qualitative leap, and the first-order transcendent space of the death wish is driven into reflexivity, generating those historically new formal structures and second-degree textual solutions which are the various modernisms. Thus Barthes has observed that

> the greatest modernistic works linger as long as possible, in a sort of miraculous stasis, on the threshold of Literature itself, in this anticipatory situation in which the density of life is given and developed without yet being destroyed through its consecration as an [institutionalized] sign system.[8]

By this suspension, in which representation undermines itself, modernism hopes to preserve and to keep open the space of some genuine Experience beyond reification, the space of that libidinal and Utopian gratification of which the Frankfurt School speaks, a space in which the failure of imagination, cancelled by the form itself, can then release the imaginary to some more intense second-degree fulfillment and narrative figuration. Barthes, in-

8. Roland Barthes, *Writing Degree Zero*, translated by Annette Lavers and Colin Smith (London: Jonathan Cape, 1967), p. 39, translation modified.

deed, goes on to evoke Proust, "whose whole work constitutes a simultaneous movement towards, and withdrawal
from, Literature." The Proustian solution is exemplary in
its twin evocation and cancellation of immediate experience, which remains empty and a dead letter until, in that
second time which is the time of writing and expression, it
finally takes place "in reality" as though for some "first
time." Yet in another sense, for Barthes, none of the
modernist "solutions" are exemplary, for each is a unique
and unstable, ad hoc improvisation which desperately de-
nies its formal preconditions in order to project some more
authentic space beyond them. But in the reified world, this
ultimate Utopian fulfillment finds only the space of the
Thanatos open all around it and must seek its *jouissance* in
the place of second death.

The Human Age is yet another such idiosyncratic and
unstable formal subterfuge, unique above all, perhaps, in
that it thematizes this dialectic as such and identifies the
deathly character of its solution. Yet it would be wrong to
think that this solution—the material beyond of a theological science fiction drawn back into mortal history—spells
an end to the contradictions that generated it. On the contrary, it now renews them in the ultimate crisis of Lewis'
narrative system. For if the second death is an imaginative
possibility, and death can become real after all, then the
satirist bears final responsibility for what are now real
victims, and the guilt inherent in his aggressivity must at
last be confronted undisguised.

In this sense, all of Lewis' works are both expressions
of violence and implicit meditations on its source and consequences. From the duel in *Tarr* and the murder in
Snooty Baronet to the criminal irresponsibility of *The Revenge for Love*, the wanton executions of the Bailiff in *The
Childermass*, the sadistic tortures of Sammael's penal system, and beyond, even to that gigantic angel's foot which
squashes Pullman at the end of the first, radio version of
the otherwise unfinished *Human Age*, these works are

punctuated by mortal assaults of which the following episode may stand as an emblem:

> In the roadway Satters grasps in both his hands the funny human plaything [a peon], gazing wildly down at it, but with the fierceness and strength of a large athletic rat it struggles, bucking and doubling itself in half upon his thigh. A sharp howl goes up from Satters as the teeth of this refractory monad are fleshed in his hand, and he drops it stamping with pain, both hands tightly squeezed between his legs. . . . The insurgent elf has rolled nimbly away and now recovering its feet it starts to run up the road away from the scene of its contretemps. 'I'll get you!' shouts Satters, and his massive body electrified with rage he whirls round and hurls himself in pursuit. 'Satters! Satters!' barks Pullman at his heels. But in a few strides Satters is up with the fugitive and with a flying kick dashes it forward upon its face, then before Pullman can reach him the football stogies are trampling it in an ecstasy of cruelty beneath them into an inert flattened mass. 'You swine!' Pullman pants as he stops before him and turns away as he sees the mangled creature stamped out of human recognition. (*CM*, 107–108)

Yet this is, as Elliott shows us, the very aim of all satire, to blast its victim with the magic of the curse:

> Proserpina Salvia, I give thee the head of Plotius. . . . his brow and eyebrows, eyelids, and pupils, I give thee his ears, nose, nostrils, tongue, lips, and teeth, so he may not speak his pain; his neck, shoulders, arms, and fingers, so that he may not aid himself; his breast, liver, heart, and lungs, so he may not locate his pain; his bowels, belly, navel, and flanks, so he may not sleep the sleep of health. . . . May he most miserably perish and depart this life![9]

We have already stressed the autoreferential dimension of such episodes in Lewis, the way in which the apparent closure of some official representation proves laterally to

9. Robert C. Elliott, *The Power of Satire* (Princeton: Princeton University Press, 1960), p. 288.

designate the process by which the representation has itself been constructed. Nor were the polemic works excluded from this process: we have examined the peculiar turn by which these cultural critiques, themselves cultural products, found themselves attacking culture itself; themselves the work of intellectuals, attacking intellectuals; by which these theories of *ressentiment*, denouncing it in their objects, were themselves products of *ressentiment*.

That Lewis was in some sense himself aware of this contradiction is amply documented by his most complex and reflexive satiric construction, *The Apes of God*. This work, in one sense little more than an episodic cage-by-cage exhibition of all the varieties of the Bloomsbury "apes," nonetheless explicitly raises the structural issue of the vantage point from which they may reliably be observed and described: a privileged consciousness presumably itself immune to ridicule, which is however fatally drawn into its own exhibits after the now-familiar pattern of the "satirist satirized" ("what is the use of a mirror then if it reflects a World, always, without the principal person—the Me?"). Thus we are given to witness the "education," the initiation into the world of the Apes, of the imbecilic young would-be poet Dan Boleyn by his mysterious patron, Sir Horace Zagreus. We believe what Dan sees because he is innocent enough to register the noxious assaults of these improbable and artificial personages, which he would in any case be incapable of inventing in his own right; and we believe Sir Horace's running commentary on the spectacle because Dan does; and because, being himself hostile to the Apes, Sir Horace must necessarily be different from them, and as a non- and anti-Ape therefore presumably a positive figure; and finally because Sir Horace is himself but the mouthpiece and spokesman for the even more mysterious ideologue Pierpoint, who never appearing within the work, is thus effectively preserved from the operation of its corrosive satire.

In the end, however, his round of visits complete, Dan is himself expelled into outer darkness on the grounds that he is, in Sir Horace's opinion, little better than an Ape himself. With this reversal, the reality of Sir Horace is suddenly called into question as well, now coming before us as a kind of minor Bloomsbury Charlus as corrupt and artificial as everyone he has so assiduously denounced. We begin to wonder, moreover, whether the whole spectacle has not been somehow prearranged in advance by Zagreus, and through him, by the absent but all-powerful Pierpoint; whether these ostensible enemies of the unreal are not in fact themselves the secret fomenters and promoters of such unreality for purposes known only to them, just as the Bailiff—officially the Minos of the afterworld and the judge of souls on the basis of their "personality"—proved to be the very agent and instigator of the immaturity he was called upon to judge.

Thus the work unravels itself and undermines its own first principles, in a kind of narrative version of phenomenological bracketting which holds this universe of representation open to us only so long as its baleful inventory requires, thereupon abolishing itself in turn and dismissing its own point-of-view figures into the hell they had prepared for other people. Yet the execution of the satirists themselves fails to revive their victims.

Nor can Lewis be said to have been unaware of these paradoxes on the polemic level either, where his aggressivity seems at length on the point of turning on himself and on his own practice:

> The volume of dogmatic abuse directed more generally at the 'intellectual'. . . . is, in the nature of things, a volume of bitter words issuing from the pens and the typewriting machines of 'intellectuals' —but of 'intellectuals' who have a grudge against the intellect, because the intellect has not served them as well as it should, and has brought them

neither fame nor money.—But a great deal of this
abuse is deserved—if you allow the term 'artist',
or 'intellectual', a wide and popular enough interpretation. These gentlemen are in fact drawing upon
their wide and intimate knowledge, and merely abus-
ing *themselves*. There is no target so good for a
bull's-eye as that inside one's own breast.[10]

So Lewis seems to hover on the brink of a momentous
discovery, as he contemplates a sham world filled with unreal puppets who can nonetheless be killed. Yet the agents
of such death are themselves unreal, perhaps even more so
than their victims. Such is the burning political message of
The Revenge for Love: out of the realm of the shades, out
of the paper world of false faces and hollow effigies, walking caricatures, split-men, scarecrows and automata, from
out of Bloomsbury, out from among the Hardcasters and
the Abershaws, the fake world of millionaire reds and
armchair bolshevik intellectuals, there issues at length a
force to kill the living. What does not exist reaches out its
shadow arm to strike down real flesh and blood, and, itself
insubstantial, to leave real corpses behind it. Paper weap-
ons that cut down real bodies: what better description of
the baleful influence of the political intellectual himself?
Yet it is a self-portrait, for was not Lewis himself just such
an intellectual, whose endless and enthusiastic pages, like
those of a Brasillach or a Roy Campbell, of a Céline or a
Drieu la Rochelle, could be invoked to legitimize the most
mindless forms of brutality and institutional lynching? So
at length the "satirist satirized" takes its definitive, unwit-
ting, and at the same time curiously self-conscious form, as
Lewis denounces himself in the person of the Marxist
enemy, lending him (in *The Revenge for Love*) his own dis-
carded surname (Percy).

Not the crimes themselves, indeed, are what is here
condemned: not the mindless executions, the sheer blood-

10. Wyndham Lewis, *Men Without Art* (London: Cassell, 1934), pp. 279–
280.

guilt alone, which any garden-variety gangster or torturer could provide, and which it would not require Lewis' genius to arraign. No, it is rather the essential "innocence" of intellectuals which is here in question: this private inner game of theoretical "convictions" and polemics against imaginary conceptual antagonists and mythic counterpositions, of the monad's projection of its own shadow sign systems upon the historical struggles of living people, of passionate private languages and private religions, which, entering the field of force of the real social world, take on a murderous and wholly unsuspected power. So the fascist theoreticians of the twenties and thirties, many of them quite genuinely shocked to discover the things for which the words really stood; so the postwar generation of American liberal theoreticians, elaborating enthusiastic apologias for the "free world" and exulting in the ingenuity of their own paper strategy and contingency planning, which were at length to realize themselves in the smoking and bleeding genocide of South-East Asia. Not that they meant that, exactly, for it is precisely this reality isolation of the intelligentsia of power, it is precisely its blind imprisonment in its own world of words, which is at issue. That was not our fault; that was not what we had in mind at all! It is, indeed, to "rue" such terrible innocence that on the closing page of *The Revenge for Love*, before our astonished eyes, there hangs and gleams forever the realest tear in all literature.

Appendix /
HITLER AS VICTIM

HE SLAPDASH SERIES OF NEWSPAPER
articles in which Lewis conveyed his im-
pressions of Berlin immediately after the
first great Nazi victories in the Reichs-
tag in September 1930, and which were
published as *Hitler* (London: Chatto &
Windus, 1931), are as notorious as they are unread: the
following brief account of this work, whatever its general usefulness, will indeed lead us to some unexpected
conclusions.

With his satirist's feeling about cities, Lewis could
hardly omit an initial tableau of Berlin ("Chicago, only
more so if anything, but minus Bootleg, and with that
great difference—that politics account for much of the
street violence" [18]). The political point made here is that
Nazi street violence is essentially a reaction to Communist
violence and provocation; yet the inevitable narrative point

is rather different: "But elegant and usually eyeglassed young women will receive [the tourist], with an expensive politeness, and he will buy one of these a drink, and thus become at home. . . . Then these bland Junos-gone-wrong, bare-shouldered and braceleted (as statuesque as feminine show-girl guardees) after a drink or two, will whisper to the outlandish sightseer that they are *men*. . . ." (24). With this characteristic and obsessive motif out of the way, we come to the political analysis proper, which I will resume as a series of theses:

1. "Adolf Hitler is just a very typical german 'man of the people'. . . . As even his very appearance suggests, there is nothing whatever eccentric about him. He is not only satisfied with, but enthusiastically embraces, his *typicalness*. So you get in him, cut out in the massive and simple lines of a peasant art, the core of the teutonic character. And his 'doctrine' is essentially just a set of rather primitive laws, promulgated in the interest of that particular stock or type, in order to satisfy its especial requirements and ambitions, and to ensure its vigorous survival, intact and true to its racial traditions" (31–32). This is very different from the hero-worshipping tones with which Pound salutes Mussolini's "genius"; it also conveys the stance of Lewis' articles. He means to convey the spirit, to the British public, of a phenomenon culturally alien to it; he intends to translate and to explain the Nazi movement as a matter of some historical significance, but not necessarily to endorse it. "It is as an exponent—not as critic nor yet as advocate—of German National-socialism or Hitlerism, that I come forward" (4). It seems to me that this didactic stance is essential in grasping the symbolic value Hitler (and Germany) had for Lewis: not only are they doubly oppressed—by Marxist provocation and by the Versailles Treaty—but this oppression is formally inscribed within his text as the misunderstanding and miscomprehension of the British reader, against which Lewis must write.

2. The Nazi conception of race is a welcome antidote to the Marxian conception of class: "The Class-doctrine— as opposed to the Race-doctrine—demands a *clean slate*. Everything must be wiped off slick. A sort of colourless, featureless, automaton—*temporally* two-dimensional—is what is required by the really fanatical Marxist autocrat. Nothing but a mind *without backgrounds*, without any spiritual depth, a flat mirror for propaganda, a parrot-soul to give back the catchwords, an ego *without reflection*, in a word a sort of Peter Pan Machine—the adult Child—will be tolerated" (84).

3. Hitler's program is exemplary as a defense of Europe, at a time when Europe's intellectuals are at work undermining its legitimacy through their "exotic sense" (a "sentimentalizing with regard to the Non-White World" [121]). In effect, the Hitlerist has this message for the ruling classes of other European countries: "When, respected sir, and gracious lady, are you going—oh short-sighted, much indulging, sentimentally-renegade person that you are!—when may we hope that you will turn for a change to more practical interests? How about giving your White Consciousness a try for a little—it is really not so dull as you may suppose! A 'White Australia'—that may be impracticable. But at least there is nothing impracticable about a 'White Europe'. And today Europe is not so big as it was. It is 'a little peninsula at the Western extremity of Asia'. It is quite small. Why not all of us draw together, and put out White Civilization in a state of defense? And let us start by mutually cancelling all these monstrous debts that are crushing the life out of us economically" (121).

4. The Nazi program recapitulates many of Lewis' most deeply felt polemic themes: "A 'Sex-war', an 'Age-war', a 'Colour-line-war', are all equally promoted by Big Business to cheapen labour and to enslave men more and more. I do not like the present Capitalist system" (97). Hitlerism not only repudiates the call to hatred and divi-

sion of Marxian class war, and the pernicious "trahison des clercs" of the "exotic sense," it also gives the welcome example of a transformation of Western "youth cults" into a genuine political movement (97).

5. "Race" essentially stands for the affirmation of the specificity of the national situation: this is the sense in which Lewis deals with Nazi antisemitism. The latter is, according to him, a German national characteristic, however unlovely, and must be understood as such. But here Lewis has a counter-sermon for the Germans themselves, as they try to explain themselves to other nations: "The Hitlerite must understand that, when he is talking to an Englishman or an American about the 'Jew' (as he is prone to do), he is apt to be talking about that gentleman's *wife!* Or anyhow *Chacun son Jew!* is a good old english saying. So if the Hitlerite desires to win the ear of England he must lower his voice and coo (rather than shout) *Juda verrecke!* if he *must* give expression to such a fiery intolerant notion. Therefore—a pinch of malice certainly, but no 'antisemitism' for the love of Mike!" (42).

6. Hitlerian economics are those of the German peasant, essentially an anticapitalist attack on banks, loancapital, and the War Debt. Hitler is a "Credit Crank." The Nazi opposition to Communism ("which has taken the mechanical ways of Megalopolis into the villages") "attacks the substitution, by the Communist, of the notion of quantity for that of *quality*. . . . Upon some points, of course, the Communist and the Nationalsocialist are in considerable agreement. Ultimately, the reason why their two doctrines could never fuse is this: the Marxist, or Communist, is a fanatically dehumanizing doctrine. Its injunctions are very rigidly erected against the continuance of 'the person'. In the place of 'the person' the Communist would put the thing—quantity in place of quality, as it is stated above. . . . So, even if Hitlerism, in its pure 'germanism', might retain *too much* personality, of a second-

rate order, nevertheless Hitlerism seems preferable to Communism, which would have *none at all,* if it had its way. Personality is the only thing that matters in the world" (182–183). Thus, "the *Weltanschauung* of the Hitlerist or his near-relation (the egregious 'Credit-Crank') is laughing and gay compared to that of his opponent, the Communist. . . . On principle—for his is a deliberately 'catastrophic' philosophy (the word is Marx's)—the Communist views everything in the darkest colours. . . . The Hitlerist dream is full of an imminent classical serenity— leisure and abundance. It is, with them, *Misery-spot* against *Golden Age!"* (183–184).

Most discussions of this book (which is generally passed over in embarrassed silence) have centered on the false problem of whether, on the strength of this "misguided" assessment of Hitler before he came to power, Lewis is to be thought of as a fascist or fascist sympathizer. The reader is generally reminded that Lewis changed his mind, and on the eve of World War II wrote an anti-Nazi counter-blast, *The Hitler Cult and How It Will End* (1939). But Lewis' opinion of Hitler is by no means the most significant feature of the earlier work.

What is essential from our point of view is that *Hitler* is informed by *all* the ideological positions which will remain constant to the very end of Lewis' life: those fundamental themes do not change, even if his view of Hitler did. Among them, and far more central than his attitude towards Hitler as a historical figure, is his attitude towards *fascism* as a historical force. Here, but to the end of his career, fascism remains for Lewis the great political expression of *revolutionary* opposition to the status quo. This fundamentally historical vision of fascism—this structural place of "fascism" in Lewis' libidinal apparatus—is not altered by his later (and impeccable) anti-Nazi convictions, and is in fact recapitulated in *Monstre gai,* published only two years before Lewis' death in 1957:

> Hyperides represented the most recent political
> phenomenon—hated or disliked by everybody. Here
> was the Fascist, the arch-critic of contemporary soci-
> ety. On earth this newcomer proposed to supplant
> the enfeebled Tradition, of whatever variety, no
> longer able to defend itself. So this enfeebled Power
> of Tradition, and its deadly enemy, the Marxist
> Power, joined forces to destroy this violent Middle-
> man (a borrower from both the new and the old).
>
> (*MG*, 220)

Coming in the midst of the Cold War, and after the utter
annihilation of Nazism as a presence on the world political
scene, this retrospective evaluation of World War II may
seem anachronistic, and the reader may be tempted to see
it as a tired survival of thoughts that were alive for Lewis
in the 20's and 30's. Yet the fact that fascism continued to
stand as the political (and libidinal) embodiment of Lewis'
chronic negativity, his oppositionalism, his stance as the
Enemy, long after the defeat of institutional fascism itself,
may, I think, be better grasped from a somewhat different
perspective. The figural value of fascism as a reaction is
determined by the more central position of Communism,
against which the anticapitalist posture of protofascism (of
which Lewis approved) must always be understood. We
have touched on a number of reasons why Communism
could not, for Lewis, be a satisfactory solution. The ultimate one now proves to be his feeling—paradoxical after
all that has been said—that Communism was a historical
inevitability, and thus, in a sense, the final and most irrevocable form of the *Zeitgeist*, that against which the oppo-
sitional mind must somehow always take a stand.

In this sense, and in the spirit of the present study,
which has been an *immanent* analysis of Lewis' works, dis-
engaging the self-critique always structurally implicit in
them, we may allow his own truth-in-jest to have the final
word:

> I know that at some future date I shall have my niche
> in the Bolshevist Pantheon, as a great enemy of the

Middle-class Idea . . . I say: "I shall be among the bolshie prophets!" My "bourgeois-bohemians" in *Tarr*—and oh, my *Apes of God!*—will provide 'selected passages' for the schoolchildren of the future communist state,—of that I am convinced—to show how repulsive unbridled individualism can be.[1]

1. Wyndham Lewis, *Men Without Art* (London: Cassell, 1934), pp. 267–268.

Index /

187

Check Out Receipt

McKinley Park

Saturday, February 5, 2022 1:29:34 PM

Item: R0401070620
Title: This is ecstasy
Due: 2/26/2022

Item: R0024608707
Title: Fables of aggression :
Wyndham Lewis, the modernist as fascist
Due: 2/26/2022

Item: R0335910152
Title: Il decameron
Due: 2/14/2022

Item: R0092521898
Title: Blind Willie McTell, 1929-1933
Due: 2/26/2022

Total items: 4

Branch Hours:
Mon. & Wed. 12-8
Tues. & Thur. 10-6
Fri. & Sat. 9-5
Sunday 1-5

1443

Designer	Eric Jungerman
Compositor	Typesetting Services of California
Printer	Braun-Brumfield
Binder	Braun-Brumfield
Text	VIP Plantin
Display	Typositor Gill Sans Bold Condensed
Cloth	Holliston Roxite B 53525
Paper	50 lb. Warrens